CW00429866

Eddie Williams
18/6/58

Thomas Cook
harrwde
WC SOLL 102 607
0844 8798372

a question of dharma

DAVID SMITH

a question
of dharma

108 Questions and Answers
on Practising the Buddhist Path
to Liberation

ALOKA PUBLICATIONS

Published by
Aloka Publications
email: alokapub@dharmamind.net
web: dharmamind.net

© David Smith 2008

Printed in England by BookPrintingUK.com
Design James Ferguson

British Library Cataloguing in Publications Data:
A catalogue record of this book is available from the British Library

ISBN 978-0-9542475-2-2

The right of David Smith to be identified as the author of this work
has been asserted by him in accordance with the Copyright,
Design and Patents Act 1988

Contents

About the Author

David Smith was born in 1946 in Oxford, England. His Buddhist training began over 30 years ago, in Zen. He practised for six years with the late Venerable Myokyo-ni, a teacher from the Rinzai school, at the Buddhist Society in London. He then went to Sri Lanka and lived there for three years as a Theravada novice monk. It was while he was in Sri Lanka that his spiritual breakthrough took place, and it is this that forms the framework of his first book, *A Record of Awakening*, published in 1999.

Returning to England, he went back to his occupation as a gardener. Greatly inspired by the direct non-conceptual approach found in Zen and Dzogchen, which also mirrors his own understanding of the Dharma, David says the spirit of that training has never left him. Now that he has turned to Dharma teaching, he leads a traditionally inspired yet non-sectarian Dharma group that has at its very basis the cultivation of that non-conceptual spirit. Its practice framework is within the all-embracing spirit of Mahayana Buddhism.

David leads regular weekly and monthly meetings as well as residential retreats with his DharmaMind group. He is also a guest leader of retreats around Britain and abroad, and the author of a second book, *Dharma Mind Worldly Mind*, published in 2002.

Acknowledgements

I would like to take this opportunity to express my gratitude to three people for their commitment in helping make this book possible. First, I'd like to thank Catherine Baker for her single-minded application in compiling and editing this work, and without whose effort this book would not have been created. My gratitude also goes to James Ferguson for the superb cover design which includes the line-drawing of the Manjusri Buddha image found on the Dharmamind Buddhist Group website, and to Carey Hendron for her time and patience in copy-editing. Finally, my gratitude also goes to the Tibetan Lama Ato Rinpoche for taking the time to read my manuscript and recommending it to readers.

Editor's Note

Over a period of five years, from 2002 to 2007, most of the questions and answers reproduced in this book were posted on the Forum page of the DharmaMind Group website (www.dharmamind.net). The DharmaMind Group teacher is David Smith (see About the Author). A number of the 108 questions appearing here were posted to the website by people who have attended David's retreats and are familiar with the 'practice of no-practice' that he teaches. Other questions come from people who are new to the practice and, because of their experiences with it, want to know more. Some just question out of curiosity. It adds up to a rich variety of questions that are directly and simply expressed, and together reflect the experiences of numerous Dharma-farers. We can identify with so many of the questioners. By the same token, David's responses to the questions are highly accessible to the reader, reflecting his living experience as they do, and his own inimitable brand of humour.

Both questions and answers have been edited, for clarification only. Their division into nine sections is, necessarily to some extent, arbitrary. Of course on the website they appear in order of the date posted, and so are random in regard to content. The idea to produce them in book form meant that some structure had to be imposed. As I went through the editing process, it seemed to me that most of David's responses to the questions reflected certain key themes I have heard him come back to again and again during retreats and other Dharma-teaching situations. So the section titles refer not to the questions so much as to the answers.

This applies particularly to Sections 2 to 9. As its title suggests, the first section is more wide-ranging, serving as a useful general reference to David's teaching.

Question 1 and its response have been repeated at the beginning of Section 6, not because of an oversight, but because as an introduction to this book and as an introduction to Section 6, I thought it was equally valuable. It bears repeating.

Catherine Baker
Birmingham 2007

Introduction

What I would consider to be one of the most outstanding qualities of Buddhism is that among its great variety of schools a practice can be found that is suitable for any individual aspiring to the self-transforming process that is the Dharma. From the manifold schools and practices of Tibetan Buddhism to the simple and direct approach of Zen, from the orthodox approach of Theravada, and its adherence to the Pali Canon, to the latest interpretations of the Canon's practices, exemplified by the no-frills approach of the revitalized vipassana techniques – every type of disposition is catered for.

The last few centuries have seen many new schools arising in the Far East, and now that Buddhism has come to the West, attention is being given to amalgamating many of the traditional practices into one package, to create what is quickly becoming known as Western Buddhism. If this is not enough to tempt us, there is also a growing body of practitioners here in the West who are not content to work with a tried and tested tradition, but rather put together their own independent form of Dharma practice, based upon picking and choosing from various traditions, to create what they consider to be the practice best suited to their needs.

What this book shows, with its questions being submitted from practitioners from a variety of traditions, is that despite our chosen path there is one thing that unites us all – and that is the human condition. The habits, desires, aversions and fears that we all experience are exposed in these questions, clearly reflecting our conditioned nature as we struggle to stay on the spiritual path, as we struggle for freedom.

So whether you have, for example, a Zen practice or a vipassana one (often considered to be on opposite ends of the spectrum of practice), I hope you will be able to relate to many of the questions in this book. I hope that if you do see yourself and your own personal struggle in these questions, you will reflect on the answers and so bring a little more clarity to your understanding of the path, in sitting meditation and daily life. I believe that most of my answers are neutral in the sense they are not pointing so much at specific practices or traditions, but at the general experience of practice common to us all.

My own practice, of over 30 years' duration, has been very much inspired by the direct non-conceptual approach found in Zen and Dzogchen. I first experienced Zen at the very beginning of my Dharma training and the spirit of that training has never left me. I now lead a traditionally inspired yet non-sectarian Dharma group that has at its very basis the cultivation of that non-conceptual spirit. This spirit does not adhere to any sort of developmental path characterized by steps of refinement through various practices, but rather focuses in a simple yet courageous way directly on our true nature, our Buddha nature.

We do not try to develop anything. Rather, we learn to let go of what we already have, which are the habits and fears that have forever bound us. In so doing, we slowly wake up to what we truly are, beyond this bondage. We aspire to awaken to what I call the Dharma Mind, the mind that is our innate, pure and free nature – the mind of non-attachment.

When introducing new students to the DharmaMind Group's sitting practice, my instructions are quite brief. First, I always remind them of the importance of good posture. Whether we sit cross-legged on the floor in trad-itional style, use a kneeling stool or sit on a chair, it is important that we sit straight and balanced. Then, turning to the meditation 'technique', we begin by bringing our awareness into the body and focusing below the navel, in the area known as the hara. Once here, we concentrate on the rise and fall of the abdomen as we breathe quite natu-rally. Staying here, we develop a one-pointed concentrated mind. When this concentrated mind is established, we allow our awareness, which up till now has been focused on the one point, to let go of itself and 'fill out'. Now the experi-ence becomes one of awareness of the whole body, as well as the feelings and emotions – just awareness of the experi-ence, without judgements or reactions. It is like a mirror that sees and knows but doesn't engage with what it sees and knows. We then allow our awareness to 'fill out' still further, through the rest of consciousness, to embrace the outside environment, again without judgements or reactions, just knowing. Learning to abide in this open spacious environment allows us to get a taste of our still, open, unconditioned true nature. Our everyday awareness that we've always been familiar with is seen with ever-growing conviction as being none other than our true nature itself.

I finish my introduction to practice by pointing out that in aspiring to freedom we have to learn to take this growing familiarity with openness, with undiscriminating awareness, into the rest of our lives. Whether we are sitting, standing, walking or lying down, commitment to the training in all four postures is crucial. To take the stillness and openness of awareness into everyday life will awaken us to our true nature in the most direct way possible. As we awaken to our true nature more frequently and for longer periods of time, we eventually attain the lightness and spaciousness of being we all so much desire.

The above is a necessarily brief description of a profound process. Greater detail regarding the way of practice can be found in my responses to most of the 108 questions that follow.

There is one concept that occurs several times in this book, in both questions and in answers, that I would like to clarify – that of 'pure awareness'. This term is often used to describe the non-conceptual practice that I've touched upon above. 'Pure awareness' describes awareness that is free of judgements, of doing and attachment, pointing directly at its free, spacious and empty nature. I like to think of 'pure awareness' as being the generic name for the non-conceptual practices of Buddhism, which include both Zen and

Dzogchen, although neither tradition uses the term to describe itself or any of its practices.

Whilst thinking about a name to give to the DharmaMind group's sitting practice I found that to give a specific name to the 'practice of no-practice' would be to limit its spirit and meaning. A name of any sort would create unavoidable limitations by creating an object, thus placing the meditation in a box and suggesting a doer who has something to achieve. So the DharmaMind group doesn't have a name for its meditation practice, but rather identifies itself by expressing the spirit of practice as one of complete openness in all situations, an aspiration to '*awaken to the Dharma mind, and recognize our true nature.*' So when you come across the term 'pure awareness' in this book, please understand it as a term of convenience, for communication purposes only, pointing to the empty nature of awareness rather than any specific 'technique' or practice in itself.

Finally, the number of questions to be included in this book, when finally totted up, came to 108. This number has significance in Buddhism and several other world religions and is regarded as being auspicious, even sacred. Its origin is probably Vedic, but in Buddhism its most well-known reference is to the 108 marks found on the Buddha's footprint. There are also 108 beads on a mala. So let's hope the traditionally auspicious nature of this number transmits itself to you the reader, and may it help, support and guide you to freedom and liberation from samsara!

David Smith
Bearwood 2007

Perspectives on Dharma Practice

Q1. [This question also opens Section 6, for the reason given in the Editor's Note, page xi.] *I have attended some Sunday practice days and a week long retreat with you, but I am still unsure as to what practical aspects of meditation you are teaching. Are you teaching the noble eightfold path, four noble truths, etc., as the means to liberation, or a combination of the different traditions you have practised in? For example, your website talks a lot of 'pure awareness', but my understanding of the Buddha's teaching is that meditation practice and insight are cultivated by the eightfold path, i.e., establishing oneself in the precepts, developing awareness and concentration initially by breath awareness and then by mindfulness of the four elements of experience taught in the* Satipatthana Sutta, *while developing right thought and right view with an aim of developing equanimity (with the awareness) through the insight of impermanence, unsatisfactoriness and non-self? Could you explain how similar your teaching is to the many vipassana traditions practising from the Suttas, with their emphasis on both awareness and equanimity (and thus right view) as the means to liberation?*

.. conventional so-called devel-
all the features you describe are
..ed. This as we all know is revealed
..ctly in the Pali Canon. The Canon is
..hodox Buddhism, and is practised and
..y by the Theravada tradition. But there is a
..ithout getting involved with the controver-
s..   ..round this alternative way, it is in fact the bedrock ..   ..en, and is the pinnacle of the manifold practices of
Tibetan Buddhism known as Dzogchen. The teachings of
the so-called sudden path (such a misleading and misunderstood name, for it invariably takes years of committed practice to arrive at this 'sudden' awakening!) also go back to the
beginning of Buddhism, but these teachings are barely
touched upon in the Canon.

Rather than cultivate one by one the numerous skilful
means on offer with the highly-conceptualized gradual
path, the sudden path, so to speak, 'leaps' over them all and
positions itself at the door of awakening – the same door
that the developmental path will lead you to, because there
is only one path and one door to awakening.

It is crucial here to accept that each of us has Buddha
nature, and therefore we all possess the innate qualities of
awakening. If we can accept this, then we have the starting
point, from which all we then need to do is wake up to what
we really are. I don't want to get into a long description to
validate this form of practice, but I do want to emphasize
that to awaken to our true nature we need only to learn how
to drop the veil that is separating us from it.

We learn through deepening wisdom (non-attachment) over many years to let go of that veil, which is nothing other than a collection of habits built up and embraced by that phenomenon called 'self'. This letting go is done through uncluttered awareness, slowly becoming awake to the stillness, spaciousness and brightness of just seeing. Such experience is to taste our true nature. We then learn to abide in this profound state still more, in that bare open experience of our true nature. This is not at all easy. We need support and guidance to become more familiar with this profound state. It is the state that leads us to the direct uprooting of our dualistic mind and liberation through awakening.

If we look very carefully at this practice, we will discover all the features that you describe above. To give you just one example: the stillness that reflects your natural unborn stillness is only possible because of – even if only for a short time – 'practising' ethics, concentration, and wisdom – i.e., the eightfold path. When your mind is still, open and receptive, are your ethics not perfectly in place? Is your concentration not perfectly in place also? Without long training and learning to let go of the world that we are normally caught up in, how would it be possible to have this ability to be still? So is it not the presence of wisdom (non-attachment) that is making this experience possible? Here is the direct experience (like the analogy of the ice cream described elsewhere). It is the direct experience of the moment before thinking, before even the conceptual formula of the eightfold path comes into being. Look at this experience closely. Before conceptualization, all eight steps of the path can be seen, not just on their own, but each step supporting all the others. Each step is seen to be actually penetrating each of the others, thus becoming the one direct living experience, before that concept of the 'eightfold path' arises. The eightfold path is said to be the fourth noble truth, but actually the middle way is the true meaning of the fourth truth. The middle way is not a formula, but the direct experience of going beyond the pull of the dualistic world and living in the now. And living in the now is when you directly experience the taste of the ice cream, before the world arises.

The two ways of sudden and gradual can so easily be seen to be so far apart that many are skeptical they are the same path. But on closer examination we see they are not two at all, but rather two different ways (that suit different temperaments) along the same ancient path leading to the same ancient city.

Q2. *Could you expand on what you mean by 'cultivating the Dharma Mind', and how it differs from those teachings already available?*

A. 'Dharma Mind' is the mind that no longer is goal-orientated or fuelled by self-interest (worldly mind). To come to this point requires swimming against the current of self-interest, which cannot be done by an act of will. Instead we embark upon Dharma practice, which can be stated simply as going for refuge and pursuing the middle way (eightfold path). Through time and commitment we are no longer possessed by self-interest, but rather live life spontaneously

(selflessly) responding to what is in front of us. Or put another way, when the 'Dharma Mind' is fulfilled, we awaken
to our intrinsic pure awareness.

As for the second part of your question, the most common way to cultivate the path through developing understanding is via the eight steps of the eightfold path, generally
reduced to three main components – ethics, concentration
and wisdom. These are nurtured in various ways, depending
on the tradition and specific practices. It is the deliberate
use of these steps (often in specific stages) that allows the
unfolding of insight and the seeing of things as 'they really
are'.

We are taught in Buddhism that in order to go beyond
suffering the crucial focus must be on the fourth noble
truth and the cultivation of understanding through the
eight steps or three components. But actually it is not the
eightfold path that is at the heart of the fourth noble truth.
The middle way is at the heart. For only by walking the
middle way is it possible to go beyond eternal suffering. The
Buddha 'teased out' the middle way and systematized it into
eight steps to make it possible for most of us to understand
this ambiguous concept, to make it possible for us to begin
work on ourselves, to fulfil the promise of the fourth noble
truth.

For those that are of the mind and inclination, however, it
is possible to aspire to the fourth noble truth (and the
middle way) in a direct manner, without going down the
developmental route of using the stages and the many
conceptual practices required. Two traditions that don't

concern themselves with the 'bits and pieces' of the path are Zen and Dzogchen. Zen, for example, rather than walking through stages on the path, positions itself at the end of the path (so to speak) where all concepts and developmental stages have dropped away. Zen nurtures a fundamental spirit of openness and completeness from the beginning (sometimes called 'beginner's mind'). This I have chosen to call 'Dharma Mind'. It is like aspiring to the awakened mind right from the beginning of training, the awakened mind free from concepts, ambition and dualities, which abides in the present moment with complete openness and courage.

Q3. *How should I understand the hindrances relating to pure awareness?*
A. This is a very good example to illustrate the fundamental difference in attitude and application between the pure awareness approach to practice and the more usual approach.

With the conventional approach we see the so-called hindrances as being just that – something that we need to either avoid or deal with in order to nurture still deeper our understanding of the path. Because we see these experiences as blocking the path, we may indeed view them with some negativity and frustration and would dearly like them to clear off and stop making our practice more difficult than it already is. I suspect that it would not be too difficult to imagine they may even be sent to us from some outside agent such as mara, in order to deliberately impede the practice. Then a 'me and it' dualistic relationship becomes inevitable, and we give these hindrances a lot of attention as we work to eliminate them with the various 'skilful means' of practice available to us. But if we are committed to the pure awareness path, we have an approach to working with them that is quite radically different, even seemingly contradictory.

The pure awareness approach is revolutionary. Instead of dealing with the hindrances as described above, in cultivating 'pure awareness' or, as I like to call it, 'awakening the Dharma Mind', we actually do nothing.

Instead of perceiving these experiences as something negative and dualistic, and perhaps even not 'me' at all, we embrace everything with a spirit of openness. We do this with the clear understanding that these so called 'hindrances' are a fundamental part of ourselves that have broken off into delusion and which we are no longer prepared to be in conflict with nor enslaved by. Now we willingly accept them for what they are, without any sort of reaction whatsoever. Acceptance means that rather than buy into the reactionary habit that we have developed towards these experiences over our lifetime, we now choose to embrace and contain them instead. No longer do we think of these so-called 'hindrances' in the manner that we used to, but rather they are now seen as a golden opportunity, something to make friends with, indeed love. We now know them as fundamental parts of our make-up that somehow have broken off into dualistic conflict, and only serve the purpose of creating the karma that keeps us bound to the eternal wheel of becoming.

This accepting means that we not only resist getting carried away physically, emotionally and verbally, but we don't even mentally label the experience, for example, as being 'good' or 'bad', 'skilful' or 'unskilful'. No judgements at all. Become like a reflecting mirror that impartially reveals what comes into its field without judgement and reaction. If it becomes an emotional experience, learn to carry that emotion and hand yourself into the present moment. Most crucially, carry in your body whatever is the emotional impact, and with it, learn to function in a normal human way. Carry those 'hindrances' with a willingness and openness, and soon you will no longer be creating the karma that you once did and will cease to create the seeds of yet another unknown rebirth. Soon those so-called 'hindrances' will reveal themselves as being nothing other than the Buddha himself, as you awaken to your pure intrinsic awareness – that awareness which, not for a single moment, has ever been in conflict with or even been touched by your 'hindrances'.

Q4. *What is this 'revolutionary approach' to pure awareness you talk about? Many Buddhist traditions, and indeed contemporary organizations, teach the do-nothing, non-judgmental and accepting awareness you talked about. Non-Buddhist teachers such as Krishnamurti have also explored this 'pure awareness' approach to awakening in great detail.*

A. I do not pretend that the practice of pure awareness is something unique to Buddhism. What I mean by 'revolutionary' is that for the first time in our life we turn away from self-interest, this self-interest which is unavoidable as part of our normal human condition. We learn to surrender, and to do so not by an act of will, but rather through authentic spiritual practice. The Buddha said that taking on practice is like being carried along by the current of a stream and making the decision to turn around and swim against that current. To 'rebel' against all the conditioning that makes me what I am and replace that with the true human being. Krishnamurti himself said that giving up the self is not just another revolution – but the only revolution. We often like to talk of a revolution such as replacing capitalism with communism, but sooner or later either system will go into change. The real revolution of inner change, if done properly, lasts forever.

Q5. *Sometimes when I manage to still the mind whilst meditating, I may notice a thought arising in my awareness, and then in this same awareness perhaps a sound arises and is noticed (say a dog barking). These both simply appear as phenomena arising in my awareness, yet upon reflection I associate, or 'own' the thought, yet not the sound of the dog. I treat thoughts as being mine and can get all hot and bothered about them. But the phenomena that I 'experience' as sound, I can simply let go and not treat as belonging to me, as being outside of me. However, more and more I am coming to regard both so-called thoughts and so-called sounds as being one and the same. Just experience registering on the radar of awareness. Is this an experience of non-self, I wonder, or am I fundamentally mistaken about what is meant by self and non-self?*
A. It is non-self if mental objects and experiences are allowed to rise and pass away, and self if you grasp at them and make them 'mine'. If you see outside experiences and

inner experiences as just things on the 'radar of awareness', then the sooner you bring that understanding into your life the sooner you will go beyond suffering, but can you do that? If not, then that is where you need to focus. Throw yourself into the practice, so that you can fulfil that hint of insight. Thinking about it more won't do you much good at all.

Q6. *When I am contemplating the three aspects of reality (anicca, anatta, dukkha), I find I start off thinking and reflecting on these facts as if I was a doctor looking over my body, mind and sensations, constantly reminding myself of their true nature. However, I know the* Satipatthana Sutta *states you should observe 'body in body', 'feelings in feelings', etc. I do occasionally dissolve the separation of my observer and my observed, but find it difficult to maintain this awareness. Should I be patient and allow the awareness to naturally integrate with body and mind (which it does eventually), or should I be making more effort to contemplate less and experience more. Secondly, I've heard different meditators tend to reflect on either anicca or anatta or dukkha. My experience is that very quickly they appear as different aspects of the same truth, inseparable. What is your experience of this?*

A. After starting meditation, concentration will naturally take time to strengthen. Therefore, being more dualistic with our contemplation when concentration is at its weakest (though present to a good degree) will be our starting point. As concentration strengthens, we will then be able to fulfil the sutta's teaching of being at one with our chosen subject. It is also useful to remember that a skilful means is to arouse your insightful understanding from previous meditations and bring it to bear in the present contemplation. This should aid the development of concentration markedly. From my experience, maintaining awareness is hardly ever a passive engagement. Rather it is one that continually needs 'pumping up' through either returning briefly to your samatha practice and/or deliberately surrendering to the insightful knowledge that is present. The answer to your second question is yes, all three are characteristic of any experience after you have stepped beyond the more coarse labelling process.

Q7. *How can we go for refuge to the sangha, when the sangha is (presumably) full of unenlightened people like me? How can we go for refuge to something which is not (yet) a manifestation of ultimate truth? Is it not rather that we are going for refuge to the Ariya Sangha, meaning the sangha of the Buddha's disciples who have attained the path in full? Or is it that we go for refuge to each other's Buddha nature, its potential, rather than its reality?*
A. To go for refuge to the Ariya Sangha is an important and necessary aspect of taking refuge, for it is the Ariya Sangha that helps teach, guide and inspire us. We study their enlightened understanding of the Dharma, and through that knowledge and the inspiration that we experience we put our understanding into practice, hopefully not falling into the trap of practising the way we think we should (or would like to) practise. So, we put our understanding into practice, but where?

Of course, we have the opportunity in our daily sitting and throughout our daily activities. But we can also extend our engagement with practice to include the sangha that we belong to. We can look upon our sangha as the vehicle for our own enlightenment and use it as a support as we open up to ourselves more and more. To be with like-minded people is such an important feature of our practice. Of course, involvement with sangha is a two-way process. We need also to contribute to sangha in order for others to benefit. See your sangha as your work area within practice – to give and to take.

You would like to have the best possible support, even if those who support you are not enlightened. You would like to draw on a consistent commitment from people, people who give you strength, support and encouragement. If you appreciate these qualities that your friends aspire to, then you too need to aspire to these same qualities so that you may help them – thus recognizing the qualities of Buddha nature.

If we only take refuge in the Ariya Sangha, we run the risk of living in our heads. If we only take refuge in the unenlightened sangha, we run the risk of losing direction. Combining the two should give us a well-rounded and skilful framework for the third refuge.

Q8. *Sometimes during meditation, when I'm concentrated, a 'dot' appears within my awareness that is lighter than its surroundings. I don't want to call it light, yet its colour is 'whitish'. I wonder whether there is any significance to this, and whether, when it arises, it should become the focus for my concentration. Or should I remain attending to whatever it was that I was initially focused upon (say the rise and fall of the abdomen)?*

A. Whatever you have been taught to concentrate on during your meditation should be the sole focus of your attention. All manner of things can come into the mind at these times of concentration and if we give these experiences our attention we will soon lose any sense of one-pointed meditation. If experiences such as these persist and are bothersome, then consult your teacher.

Q9. *Lately my life has become quite hectic and stressful. Consequently, when I come to meditate I'm seeking to have a pleasant time of it and to escape for a while (so to speak). In terms of Dharma practice, is this OK? I look on it as a skilful means, giving me time out so that I can keep some sort of positive emotion going in my life.*

A. We all tend to do this when the escape brings us pleasure and a break from our reality, but at the same time we should be cautious. Hopefully, we are sitting essentially to get to the bottom of our condition and instigate change, so indulging in fantasies is not the way forward. Then again, our fantasies do point to the sort of things that go to make us up, the things that we need to get to know, so in that sense it could be justified and considered part of practice...

Q10. *As part of your answer to a recent question you said: 'We can work on fear, which manifests in countless mental and emotional forms, through the correct practice of the path'. Please could you say more about working with fear, especially when the fear seems so irrational, e.g., panic attacks, phobias, etc.*

A. For Dharma training purposes, trying to work out why we are caught by so much fear can be an unnecessary diversion. It's not usually necessary to get to the bottom of the mental pictures that fear creates and the circumstances that we are caught in, to try and figure it all out.

Fear in its 'basic' nature is emotional energy that a lot of the time is very powerful and seems to go to the very core of our being. For the most part it conditions our life and sets the parameters that we are trapped in, and is one of the reasons why so many of us never realize our potential as human beings.

There are two insights that we put in place to work with fear. These, when applied correctly, will cause the fear to cease, and the energy that creates it will return to its original nature. The two insights that we put in place to work with fear are familiarity and accepting. The reality of fear is that it can only exist by our habitual reacting to the experience of it. Cease to react, and it will die. It is that simple. But easier said than done.

The familiarity comes first. To turn away, or run away, or hit out at fear will only feed it, leading it to come back stronger than before. Do your best not to react and begin to become familiar with an experience that you've probably never looked at or stayed with. Stay with the experience, and in that staying with, accept as best as you can without reacting. Of course, this can be immensely difficult to do, if not impossible, but do your best. Develop the strength of mind and body to come back to the experience of fear over and over again. Familiarity will allow you to have the ability to come back more, and then, in accepting and containing, allowing the experience to be itself without your reacting or being carried away. This will starve the fear of the fuel of your emotional reactions, and given time it will fade away.

Q11. *When you cry, is that a failure to 'sit with' something in the hara? I suppose there are different kinds of crying and some are more emotionally indulgent than others. When I was crying about my cat I felt like I was just BEING with how much I missed him very acutely, and it felt cathartic to cry, though if I was sitting with it I guess it wouldn't feel cathartic. I'd have to sit with it?*

A. In many situations it certainly is not a failure to cry. Crying is a wonderful safety valve and one I myself have experienced several times over the years. In emotional situations during sitting practice we do our best to contain our habitual reactions, but if the emotions become too powerful then we sometimes need to 'let go'. Sometimes we need to grieve. This is necessary to be emotionally balanced, but when it crosses the line and becomes more like a self-indulgent expression of an ingrained habit, then we need to be careful.

There may be a tendency to self-indulge and feel sorry for ourselves. This can be quite an unskilful habit, so it is always good to be aware at these times. If you see that you are crossing that line, then try as best you can to resist falling into what is often an immature state. Feeling sorry for myself was a strong tendency of mine. In pulling myself out of the habit, I felt I was cultivating inner strength, allowing myself to bear with life's trials more successfully.

Q12. *Is sitting awareness the direct reflection of everyday awareness in one's life?*

A. Exactly the same, because there is only one awareness. To be able to carry the essence of what we do (or don't do!) on the cushion into the four postures and our everyday life in a seamless way, is the way to complete practice and understanding. By seeing no difference in our practice throughout the four postures of everyday life, we realize the wholeness of Dharma practice and will surely awaken from the dream of self.

Q13. *Through daily practice and just coming back to awareness of whatever's going on, I've become aware of that space you sometimes speak about, that space brought about by the spark of awareness that allows us to act rather than simply react and spin the wheel again. But I've noticed that that space isn't anything like how I expected it, I mean I've experienced it many times before, but almost sub-consciously, I didn't know what it was and I didn't pay it much attention; it was just a pause in between the daydream and the sense of purpose. But since I've been paying more attention to it, getting curious about it and trying to get familiar with that moment of anticipation and awareness, I've begun to notice that I don't experience it as simply a neutral pause but as a moment permeated with fear. So now when I'm in some comfortable daydream, fantasizing about past or future, no matter how wholesome or unwholesome it may be, I find it understandably challenging to bring myself out of a nice seemingly harmless mental drift, past a brief moment of fear and doubt and back to the reality of a cold and wet morning through which I have to walk to attend a long day of hard work. I guess this is where faith is needed, and it doesn't feel like a meaningless moment, it feels like a crucial turning point, a clear opportunity to be patient and stop spinning.*

So I guess my question is how do I find the middle way at that point, not to be too forceful and try and suppress my wandering mind, and not to be too lazy and let run it away with me? And also at what point does it become clear that this uncomfortable and often painful process of opening up to and sitting with all this dukkha I cause myself, is actually worthwhile and the best course of action?

A. Yes, there will be fear as part of the experience because you are no longer trying to control the experience in the way that you used to. Polishing awareness will encourage you to create that pause, and in the space you bring the experience, and you bring your habitual reaction. Contain all of this in a spirit of openness, and with the aid of the positive precepts continue to function in a normal and skilful way. This is the middle way. You are neither suppressing nor being carried away by the event. Finding this middle way (pure awareness practice) comes through familiarity. To come back time after time to that precious space of neither doing nor not-doing is the middle way.

By practising in this way you will inevitably experience dukkha as fear, because you are not in the familiar reactive state that reinforces the self. And you will experience dukkha because that wheel of becoming and the world that it creates is going into change, and to change the course of your karma inevitably brings negative forces within you to the surface. To me, this is the most profound act anyone can engage with because eventually it will take you beyond suffering and becoming. In my view that makes all the dukkha experienced worthwhile, especially since you will experience dukkha anyway, even if you have no practice at all. The point at which you realize this for yourself will be a part of your voyage of discovery on this wonderful path.

Q14. *In my practice of mindfulness off the cushion I find that even though my intention is to be mindful throughout the day, there are whole chunks of my day that just drift by in unmindfulness and unawareness. Can you advise on how to become more consistently awake during the day? How can I remember to be present more often?*

A. Having commitment to the practice, being willing to take this commitment into the whole of your life, without picking and choosing, gives you the platform necessary for your innate, shining, perfect awareness to be more present. I believe it is unskilful to think that the purpose of our practice is somehow to be aware all the time. This notion will set up a tension, so when we believe that we are not aware enough in our day, then we are failing; and then we begin to develop negativity. I believe authentic change and genuine understanding takes place within the framework of commitment.

Commitment not to being perfectly aware all the time, but just to come back to ourselves whenever we catch ourselves wandering off into distractions. The commitment to come back, and to come back, over and over again, with awareness of what is in front of us, is, I believe, the key to change. Practice is not about perfecting awareness! If you attach to that concept you will soon become downhearted and negative about yourself and your teachers, as this will never be achieved. 'Perfection' is nothing more than a figment of the human imagination. The great ideal of perfect awareness should be seen as something to aspire to, rather than to achieve. A valuable lesson can be learnt from contemplating this most important spiritual paradox. Simply remember, and remind yourself continually, that cultivating wholehearted commitment to practice in the four postures is the key to making yourself more awake.

Q15. *How important do you feel Dharma teachings are compared to actual personal Dharma experience through practice? Nearly all so-called Dharma groups I have attended (quite a few in different traditions) have spent lots of time talking about Buddhism and drinking tea in preference to the nitty-gritty of committed practice. Do you feel there is too much emphasis on teachings (many of which are simply philosophical discussions rather than practical support), particularly in our western culture at this time?*

A. To answer the sort of question you are asking I often use the analogy of tasting an ice cream. Imagine coming from a place that has no ice cream, and therefore a taste treat that you've never experienced. Imagine I try to describe the taste of an ice cream to you. It's cold, smooth, sweet, truly delicious. You try to imagine it, but can you really know what that taste is like, having never experienced it? No, of course you can't. There is only one way that you will know the taste of an ice cream, and that is to lick it, and at that very moment, before thinking of like and dislike, or hanging any sort of label on the experience, without theorizing in any way, you will know what an ice cream tastes like – you will know directly. This is like the practice of Dharma. We can read, listen to talks and discuss the subject till the cows come home (to make the ice cream, maybe?), but we will never really know what it is like to practice. It is only when we 'taste' the Dharma, which is to put it into direct practice and live it, that we know what the Dharma is truly about.

Although study has an important part to play in our understanding of Buddhism, there is always a great danger of over-emphasising the teachings and engaging in endless discussions. And how this plays into the hands of our western culture, with its emphasis on wanting to know all the answers to all the questions! This theorizing can also be a good diversion (conscious or not) from engaging in the direct living practice of Dharma, which tells us this is what we should be doing, this is where we have to face ourselves and all our warts. Many of us would rather think about it instead.

Q16. *Is the Sangha, one of the three precious jewels of refuge, any person who is interested in Buddhism and attends meditation classes, or is a certain level of insight required in those people before they are an object of refuge in a very confused world? How would you define the sangha?*
A. Sangha is not seen as a single person. It is a group of like-minded people, and has many functions. We humans are gregarious creatures – we seek others to join us in most things that we do in life. The way life is for most of us, with its struggles and difficulties, requires us to seek support and inspiration on a regular basis. Dharma practitioners are no different. Just to be around like-minded people is a great support and encouragement. To know that you are not the only one struggling with the realities of Dharma practice helps to keep you going.

A further advantage of sangha is to be able to 'bounce' your current understanding off others, a skilful way to hone your practice. To be tested and challenged by others is an essential feature of the path. Who you engage with in your understanding isn't really the point. Those that are more experienced than you may help with your own refinement, but engaging with those less experienced than you in turn helps them. We are all in it together to help and be helped.

These are important features of sangha, but for me there is one feature that is far and away the most important, and that is direct support in practice. By this I mean collective sitting practice (regular meetings and retreats). During these precious times we can through commitment and discipline create a supportive environment, a 'form' whereby we feel we are in the company of others seriously committed to practice.

This leads us to feel so emotionally supported that we find the courage to let go, to go beyond our perceived limitations. Whether they are physical or emotional. To let go of those perceived limits is to set in motion the changes we all want. This to me is the most important and indeed profound aspect of sangha. To let go of your habits and attachments, through courage in the knowledge that you are being supported by others doing the same, is to me quite tremendous. To break the limitations experienced in this lifetime and maybe other previous lifetimes as well, is what we practise for.

Having sangha in place whilst this change takes place shows its importance. In fact without sangha in place in our practice, the fruit that leads to liberation could never truly ripen. Taking refuge in sangha is not an option for those who want to be on the authentic path.

Q17. *How do you reconcile 'there is no meditator' with 'when you sit, know that you are sitting?'*
A. Through the letting go of the world of thought and mental pictures we arrive at a quiet place in meditation. We learn to abide in this quiet place and shortly that place becomes ever more expansive as the sense of duality slowly dissolves. Through all of this there has been a sense of seeing and knowing. Without that, we would never have arrived at this expansive and limitless experience in the first place. We then abide in just knowing. In that knowing you will find there is no one who is sitting, there is no centre and no person, just the knowing. Here we are awakening to our true nature. Our true nature is not a person and doesn't have a centre. It is a knowing that is limitless.

Here we are on the edge of the great mystery of life and death and our true nature, which is free and fills the entire universe. Dedicate yourself to the cultivation of this experience, and you will awaken to what the Buddha meant when he said these words.

Choosing the Right Path

Q18. *In your books your advice is to stick to whatever practice is taken on in a consistent way. My question is how do I know if I have a practice worth sticking to and am not heading up a blind alley as far as the spiritual life is concerned? Also, your own break-through seemed to come after you had changed your practice from Zen to Theravada. How do you reconcile this?*

A. This is one of the most difficult issues that we have to face – finding the practice that is right for our temperament, and made doubly difficult for us in the west because these days we are overwhelmed by choice. Traditionally, in the east, whatever country you were born in decided that issue for you. You just got on with whatever the indigenous tradition was. Unfortunately we don't have the luxury of not having choices.

My advice is to explore the various ways and then decide which tradition attracts you most via your inner feelings, rather than via your head. Proceed, and see how it goes. After some time you may well doubt your decision to follow that tradition and find yourself at a crossroads of carrying on or trying something else. Not easy to know what to do, but I can offer a guideline that may help.

If you are having difficulties, stay with what you have committed yourself to, stay with it and see if in a few weeks or months things get better. The problem we all have is that whatever way we decide to go there will inevitably be bottle-necks, and then we doubt the practice. Never make a decision quickly, and never when in an emotional state. Stay with it and see if the problem clears. Wait a good period of time and mull the situation over in a dispassionate way. If you still don't feel right with what you are doing, then ex-plore alternatives. Restlessness is our biggest mara and our ability to stay with difficulties our biggest challenge. A need for change may well be necessary, and by sitting with it, very often that change will take place almost of itself. Ultimately things can work out OK anyway. Change is mysterious; something can present itself quite unexpectedly if you cre-ate space for that mystery to take place, then you can slip effortlessly into the new way.

As for my experience, I think it illustrates the mystery of change, although it is admittedly an unusual example. I was happy with my Zen practice and had no thoughts of change. I went to Sri Lanka for a holiday and met a monk who in-spired me to become a monk. My initial reaction was to re-coil from that idea, but inside I knew that this was the next thing for me to do. There was no restlessness or emotional volition involved, rather an expectancy that it was the right thing for me to be doing. I considered it to be a part of a mystery that I was familiar with. This mystery is difficult to describe, but is something we all can learn to open up to and trust – with time. I have expressed my thoughts and feelings in my first book concerning this event in my life, and could best refer you to that.

Q19. *In* Dharma Mind Worldly Mind *you mention the* Satipatthana Sutta *in the chapter on awareness. What advice would you give to someone taking on the practices of the Four Foundations of Mindfulness as set forth by the Buddha in this sutta?*

A. All insight practices of Buddhist traditions have their roots in this sutta, as it lays out the path of fundamental insight that breaks the root of the delusion of self. Some insight practices may go beyond this and focus on 'what is', and Buddha nature. But 'what isn't' has first to be worked through, else the blinding notion of self will always conceal complete insight. These types of practice deal simultaneously with both of these fundamental characteristics of insight, but the removal of self-delusion step by step will always be leading. To ask about the practices in this sutta is therefore to inquire about insight practice in general and the basic framework that needs to be understood before embarking upon this form of practice. The best I can suggest is to refer you to what I have written in *Dharma Mind Worldly Mind* on the tenets, as I understand them, necessary for the insightful spiritual journey.

If at all possible find a teacher who has walked a good way down the path of insight, so that they may help you in your time of need. If you can't find one, then you will have to compromise with books and advice where you can find it, but be very careful because books and understanding their concepts can so easily be misunderstood as being all that is needed for your development, and advice from someone without sufficient understanding can lead you to confusion and even take you off the path. Next we have the essential support of sangha. It is one of the three jewels and not an optional extra. If you think you can do this practice on your own in the way it has to be done in order to enter the promise of permanent change, please forget it. You will wander off course, increase your delusion and may well get yourself into all sorts of emotional difficulties along the way. Insight practice has the power to encourage the emergence of the dark forces that are in all of us. Not knowing what to do with these forces can lead to serious problems.

Study, and put into practice the eightfold path in totality. Nurturing the eightfold path (in a direct orthodox way or a 'hidden' way, e.g., Zen) will be the active component that reveals the delusion of self, whatever method of insightful investigation you may use – including those of the *Satipatthana Sutta*.

Q20. *What would you say is the aspect of Dharma practice that westerners seem most disposed to getting wrong?*
A. To think that mixing traditions and practices is a bona fide way to practise the Dharma.

For the first time in the history of Buddhism we have (in the west) people putting together a 'universal practice'. A bit from this tradition and a bit from that tradition, until we have a practice that we have assembled and decided is the best for me. We do this not realizing that this desire to create our own practice is nearly always born of restlessness because we are unable, through lack of commitment, to stick with one way. This 'pick and mix' approach is highly suspect if you are trying to commit to a serious practice. It is true that all branches of Buddhism are growing from the same trunk, but it should be understood that the practice of Dharma by its nature is a very narrow, subtle, and transforming path. Any part of a practice that doesn't harmonize with other parts will keep you off that narrow path, and because of the inherent subtlety involved it is likely that the disharmony created will not be recognized.

Whilst sticking to the totality of a traditional way, rather than walling yourself in with your commitment, it could be considered helpful to show interest in other traditions alive in your land. Doing so may prevent conceit and intolerance. By all means show interest in the other traditions and learn from the richness of wisdom that is on offer. However, keep to one practice of one tradition, thereby ensuring you are on a tried and tested path of transformation, rather than being on one that you have, in your 'wisdom', cobbled together.

Q21. *I recently met a 'psychic' who told me that I would progress faster if I did certain types of meditations (which she would teach me of course!) that would allow me to recall 'my' previous incarnations and therefore hold onto and use the experience and knowledge that 'I' have already gained. I am curious whether you recall any of 'your' prior lives, and what you think of this advice? Thank you!*

A. This type of excursion into what we may loosely call 'new age' activities can never be thought of as useful for serious Dharma practitioners. It is so important to learn to open up to ourselves exactly where our feet are in this present moment. It is here that we get to understand ourselves, so that the potential for change can be realized. The Dharma is in the here and now, not in the past or future or in endless psychic ideas that cannot but feed mental notions and fantasies. Any practice on the path in previous lives will become a part of the subconscious framework that supports your practice in the here and now. It will be part of a wisdom that is inaccessible, and would never carry the pictures or experiences that it arose in and matured in during any past life. Let me suggest that you just forget all these 'interesting short cuts', put your nose to the grindstone, and deal with what is in front of you.

Q22. *How do you know if you are meditating too much? Too little?*
A. Not very easily is the answer to those extremes, simply because we are all different. There could be a case for too much sitting if it takes over your life, in the sense that you neglect other things that you know you should be doing in your daily routine and life in general. It could mean you may be treating meditation as an escape from your mundane reality.

It can also happen that if you sit a lot, somehow the whole process of meditation seems to grind to a halt and becomes stale. I'm not saying that if times get difficult stop sitting, but rather, if you are getting sort of possessed by meditation and becoming too detached from your experiences of life, then this is something to look at.

Too little meditation may be easier to spot. If you have an agreement with yourself to sit every day, then stick to that. That routine will soon let you know if it is too little. Sitting for just a few minutes may not be enough. If you build up to 30 to 50, even 60 minutes each sit, then this will be more than enough for a daily routine. The best way to avoid too much or too little meditation is to follow the guidance of a teacher in the tradition that, hopefully, you have chosen.

Q23. *In your opinion what is the relationship between psychological 'work', maybe termed integration, and awakening? For example, does one need to have dealt with all of one's psychological stuff before awakening happens? Or is it more the case that a reasonable level of integration is needed, which enables a steadiness of mind? From this steadiness of mind we can see how things are sufficiently for awakening to happen. Hope the question is clear.*

A. It is good to be able to dampen the idea, which many have, that sooner or later you have to go beyond all your 'stuff' and become 'perfect' before awakening can take place. I'm sure the reader will be relieved to know that you certainly do not need to have reached this lofty height – far from it in fact. Yes, it is true that we need to be reasonably balanced and integrated to be able to do this practice, but most people are. It is only a few that are not able to get themselves started. It is certainly true that much has to be transformed through practice over the years, but even quite 'heavy' karma won't necessarily 'block the path' through the final stages leading to the collapse of samsara. Through skilful practice and gradually attaining the profound state of the middle way, it is possible that many of our unresolved attachments will 'suspend', returning when the bodhisattva path is attained, providing you with rich fodder for practice that will take you through the ten stages to enlightenment.

Q24. *Do you think there is a role for psychotherapy/counselling in getting people to bring dukkha into awareness? Or do you think there are dangers, and if so what are they?*
A. If that is a useful thing to do, then why not? Counselling no doubt has many worthwhile applications, but in the context of practice? Be very careful.

For a practising Buddhist it is important to see the distinction between counselling and spiritual practice. In counselling there tends to be a specific problem or problems that are targeted by both sides and then worked upon in various ways, depending on the method used. Its ultimate success could be another issue.

With spiritual training the whole of the person is brought into view with the spirit of working on the whole person and not being side-tracked by parts of the personality that may hinder this ongoing spirit. Usually this training is done in conjunction with a teacher, but primarily the practitioner is nearly always working on himself or herself.

I think the danger is thinking that counselling is the same as a Dharma practice. It is necessary to see the completeness and non-discriminatory nature of Dharma practice in order to open to all the qualities that can be worked upon. One of its major qualities is when you truly work through a particular emotional attachment in the thorough and complete way the Dharma teaches, then that particular attachment is gone forever. I wonder if counselling can make such a similar claim?

Q25. *Quite often I come across references to the Mahayana bodhisattva ideal that suggest it is rather like being a Buddhist missionary, doing good deeds, working to save all beings from samsara. However, you seem to speak of it more in terms of being open to all of life, not discriminating in our daily experience. Do I misunderstand you? Perhaps you can say something further about how you view the bodhisattva ideal in actual practice.*

A. The stereotypical missionary work we're familiar with through our Christian culture should not be seen as having a Buddhist equivalent. The idea that Buddhists travel around trying to convert people to their beliefs simply isn't in its history or philosophy. Speaking specifically about the bodhisattva, traditionally they do help others that are in need, but they do their work because they see suffering and therefore feel a need to help. They would never pronounce that they are such beings, and try to convert others to their own beliefs.

But there is another perspective to this work alongside what we would normally perceive, which is alluded to but often misunderstood, and this points to the unique position of an enlightening being. As insight deepens the bodhisattva sees with ever-increasing clarity that all beings without exception are a product of his or her own mind, and that he or she is therefore responsible for their suffering. Bodhisattvas see that to liberate all beings from suffering, they – the bodhisattvas – must first know themselves ever more deeply. They see that to do this they also need to engage with those other beings as well as all of life (including blades of grass). For life as we know it is also a creation of the mind. It is because of this understanding, when bodhisattvas are seen to be doing good works, you are unlikely to understand the paradoxical nature of their understanding of their own lives.

With still more clarity, bodhisattvas discover that they themselves do not exist outside of other beings. So, when they finally attain liberation and pass into nirvana, all other beings are also liberated with them, (including those blades of grass), and pass into nirvana with them. Now *that* is what you would call successful missionary work!

Q26. *Meditation practice has always had a strong attraction for me, but after a few decades of meditation practice on two or three different techniques, I don't see any progress in the ability to hold steady concentration. As soon as I close my eyes, my mind becomes more active than when they are open. When I half or 3/4 close them, within a minute or so they have closed without my being aware of it, and the 'endless stream of consciousness' thought pattern has arisen. There is no rising of a single thought and watching it pass away. It is a constant stream and has always been so, from the moment I become settled on my cushion and turn inwards. With eyes open and the need to concentrate on some subject, the mind seems to behave 'normally', i.e., I have always been able to concentrate and focus and study like anyone else.*

I have done meditation on breath awareness, focusing on the heart centre, seeking the witness to thoughts, and way back in the mists of time, worked with a TM mantra for a little while. But I am seriously wondering if, after all these years, I should give up meditation as not being suitable. Have you met anyone else who experiences this kind of continuous excessive mind activity in meditation, and for so many years? Do you have any comments or suggestions?

A. It is not easy for me to make specific comments, simply because I don't know you or your practice as a whole. My reaction on reading your question was to wonder if you have focused solely on sitting meditation practice all these years, giving little attention to the rest of your day, and not looking at it through the eyes of practice?

I often come across people that have difficulty in achieving a concentrated meditation practice. Usually such people have little or no regard for practice in the rest of their daily life. To come to the meditation cushion without daily practice makes our sitting meditation shallow and one-sided. Even if we do manage to have a fairly concentrated experience, I am convinced that the fruit of such a lopsided approach will never produce anything necessary for genuine and permanent personal change.

If you care to browse through the other questions and answers you will soon see that I emphasize the importance of cultivating a practice that is not just on the cushion, but one that is visited again and again throughout the entire day. I emphasize the discovery that off the cushion the essence of practice is not at all different from on it. By cultivating the practice throughout the day, we become familiar with the central feature of coming back to ourselves, over and over again, in all situations. This allows us to begin to gather ourselves up in a more focused way, exactly as when we meditate. Because of a growing familiarity with practice, now when we come to our cushion we are at a point where we find it easier to apply extra commitment – to really gather ourselves up and enter the concentration we all aspire to in sitting meditation.

To bring practice to the whole of the day is crucial (and when I say practice, I don't mean just ethics). Practice with a teacher and a sangha. Wholeheartedly commit yourself to the Dharma, and I'm sure the expectations you have of meditation will come to be.

Q27. *I have noticed that I carry around with me different ideas or conceptual frameworks of what I am trying to do. I have also noticed that my approach can chop and change. Sometimes it may be an emphasis on metta, at other times it may be about being aware of the body, the ten precepts, or sometimes just knowing my experience. Whatever my emphasis, I usually find it helpful. I have been wondering if I am proceeding correctly. Perhaps what I am doing is just making use of the range of skilful means available to me, which are all doors into the Dharma, so this alternation doesn't matter. But sometimes I feel like I lose a sense of what I am doing, I wonder if there is a danger of becoming a jack of all trades but master of none. I would value any suggestions you may have in this area.*

A. There is nothing wrong with having various perspectives to contemplate or reflect upon. But I believe it is important that beyond this you have one main form of meditation practice that will firmly anchor you and provide the stability of practice that is crucial. Although we do have a specific meditation practice to nurture, it can be very useful to wander around and explore, hopefully in a spirit of enquiry and playfulness. Especially off the cushion. This spirit of openness helps us not to get too bogged down, and, importantly, helps us not to be always taking ourselves so seriously. It is very easy to fall into the trap that you must somehow fulfil your main practice at all costs, and as quickly as possible, that to divert is a sign of weakness or lack of commitment. As long as whatever you are contemplating is an aspect of Dharma, then you cannot ever be off the path. But always see these wonderings as a supplement to the form of practice that you are committed to.

I am aware that a lot of practitioners don't have a specific form of practice as their main focus but rather have a variety of options and choose whichever one they think is appropriate at any given time. If changing meditation practices is done with a teacher who suggests picking an option, then that is fine. But from my experience most practitioners make the choice themselves, and often for unskilful reasons, for example: Not getting anywhere, boredom, not in the right mood, etc. It is my understanding and experience that authentic understanding and change comes from learning to stay with a very specific form of practice, without diversion, usually for years. It is often the case that change takes place not because of the specific practice being cultivated, but rather through developing the ability to stay with one practice.

Q28. *Given that the pure awareness practice is meant to be a practice that one is constantly engaged with, if you find that other than managing it during a formal period of sitting, you're not managing to do it, then are you better off giving up on it altogether and* *sticking with more straightforward practices such as mindfulness of breathing and metta?*

A. If I were to give up a particular practice, I am sure it would be because it didn't feel like the right practice for me, rather than simply not being successful at it. If it doesn't feel right for you, then fine. But if you are looking for success as a criterion, then I'm not so sure about it. All forms of practice need commitment and the ability to stay with the forces that we need to stay with, as we learn to grow into something we are totally unfamiliar with. It is from this ability to grow into a practice that the changes we all desire take place. In your question you are comparing practices that may have quite sharp philosophical differences, and this is where your own disposition plays a big part, and what inspires you to take up a particular practice. With reference to the pure awareness practice, what is important to understand is that it pays no attention to any specific posture, but rather sees all of one's life as a 'seamless' whole. I hope you are practising with a teacher, for to bring pure awareness practice to the whole of your life will not be possible without one.

Q29. *My question concerns labelling experience in and out of meditation. For example, we can note our feelings, emotions and thoughts. Whether our experience is painful, pleasurable or neutral. We can also break our emotions down into the five hindrances or longer lists of mental states that exist within the Buddhist tradition. Doing this sometimes seems to help me objectify my experience and helps me notice when I am going down a certain path. At the same time I can't always define my mental states that easily, or differentiate feeling from emotion. I also experience some confusion* *as to what kind of breakdown is most helpful or necessary to practice. I would be grateful for any comments you may have in this area.*

A. This type of practice is something I'm not at all experienced with, and is not in the spirit of the DharmaMind group or website. My background is in Zen, whose spirit is not one of labelling or dissecting experience. While I do not consider myself to be a Zen practitioner these days, I have never left that spirit behind. The danger with wanting to label and compartmentalize what we are experiencing at this moment is that we can distance ourselves from the impact of the experience, and that can subtly lead us to disowning our relationship with that experience. We can take it into the realm of theory and labels rather than dealing with the emotional impact of whatever it may be. We discover through practice that in fact we spend so much of our time putting a space between ourselves and life's experiences anyway. But seeing practice as a sort of safety device that allows us to avoid the emotional reaction can create a sense of dissatisfaction and lack of fulfilment in life, because we are only living a part of it. Noting that danger, Buddhism does offer us many fine practices that do use systems of labelling and box-filling in pursuit of wisdom.

Skilful Means

Q30. *Unless I've misunderstood, the teachings on pure awareness point to its essence being shunyata. It's not a thing, an object. Therefore it can't conflict with other practices, as they are objects, upayas used to lead one and help one into pure awareness or shunyata. So if you have something that you feel is too big to sit with directly, you can use a more conceptual practice such as metta to act as a divider between 'you' and the 'something', deal with it, and then drop the metta when it's served its purpose, along with the dualism, and return to the direct experience all within the context of pure awareness.*

Please correct me on any shortcomings in the above. Now my question: When I have been taught shikantaza (just sitting), to place any emphasis, use any upaya, make any judgement, is to cease shikantaza. 'Make the slightest distinction and heaven and earth are set miles apart.' So is shikantaza or just sitting then an object, a thing, because unless I'm mistaken that statement would come into conflict with the ability of pure awareness to incorporate upayas. Obviously the aforementioned pure awareness can incorporate shikantaza, but is shikantaza simply another name for pure awareness? Can it incorporate the use of other meditation

*techniques in order to deal with seemingly unapproachable prob-
lems, or is shikantaza in itself apart from shunyata, is it nothing
more than a way in, another upaya, or object?*

A. Your overview seems to me to be correct.

From my understanding, pure awareness in its true sense
is no different from shikantaza. It is as simple and as direct as
it appears. Totally uncluttered with any kind of upaya. But
let's be realistic, and indeed pragmatic, as Master Rinzai
must have been when he introduced the koan (question)
system of meditation into his Zen teachings.

From my understanding, he too practised 'just sitting' but
realized that the mind could easily become dull and un-
interested when there was 'nothing to do' during long days
of meditation. So when he began to teach he constructed
the koan system to assist his disciples with this potential im-
passe. The system encouraged his disciples to make use of a
koan that became a (transcendental) insight tool that they
took to their cushion, as well as to the rest of their life – but
whose 'answer' was beyond the conceptual world of
dualistic thinking. He used many of these upayas, which
would systematically undermine his students' fixed experience of 'reality'. So despite apparently setting 'heaven and
earth miles apart', he too was a man with the true spirit of
Zen, in the same way that Dogen was.

I think it is very important that we in the west, and especially those of us without a mature teacher to guide us, are
realistic with the type of practice that you talk of. Yes, in its
pure form there is nothing to do but just 'be'. But there is
every likelihood that most of us westerners will never truly

be able to pull that off in a consistent way because we will be continually waylaid by the heavy karma most of us seem to be carrying around. Therefore we may wander away from the 'true path' because we have been taken over by our burden yet again through some powerful attachment that we just can't shake off. We may well then need to use a skilful means to get back on it.

What is crucial is that during these brief times when we divert, we always retain, through awareness, openness to and inclusiveness of life's experiences, which is the hallmark and spirit of the infinite path. This cannot be emphasized strongly enough. If we are always with this spirit we will not actually be off the path in any serious and damaging way, but just briefly attending to a small difficulty along the way.

Q31. *I wonder whether you can clear up some confusion I have regarding the pure awareness practice. I can relatively easily bring stillness to my mind when I meditate. The chattering mind becomes quiet and I can sit with an experience of my own presence and an awareness of the flow of my perceptions. However, there still remains a sense of 'me' doing something, i.e., being present and aware. Is this the 'pure awareness' practice that you speak about, or in 'pure awareness' should there be no longer a sense of a doer? I guess another way of posing this question is whether samatha is a prerequisite for doing the pure awareness practice? Not just concentrating the mind, but samatha in the sense of the cessation of the dualistic mind experience.*
A. Not sure what you mean by 'my own presence', but the state we are coming into is to be aware without a 'centre' – i.e., an observer. We come to this state by being able to let go

of all that comes into our experience. At first we start by bringing ourselves back from our distractions through an ever-increasing shining awareness that becomes that letting go.

Ideally you don't use any sort of 'practice'; however, you may find a samatha practice useful at times provisionally to 'get you started'. But by having some sort of 'practice', you will not be nurturing the true spirit of pure awareness, in which we are slowly becoming familiar with the subtle reality of not really doing anything at all.

This may take time to mature, so in that time we are in the state you describe. Stay there and be still; there is nothing to do, so any sense of doing something will prevent maturity. The state we are moving towards is so very subtle. It is not a state of forcing, or even of trying to find a way towards a 'goal'. Nor is it a slack state in which we become slothful and dull. We cannot create the true state. It will be there when we let go of all trying and not trying. When this profound state is present, we lose ourselves completely and become lost in our true state – our state before the 'world' comes into being – and we become the universe and all that is in it, going truly beyond time and space and birth and death.

Q32. *It is often recommended that a good degree of psychological integration and emotional positivity is achieved before taking up an insight meditation practice; that one should preferably be in a state of access concentration or dhyana and then introduce an insight 'tool'. Would you say that the same is true of the pure awareness* *practice? How might we know from our experience whether it is appropriate to take up the pure awareness practice?*

A. No, it is not the same. Pure awareness can be taken on from the first day of practice because it is not about doing or achieving anything; rather, it is about just being the way you are right now. The spirit of pure awareness is primarily about having that willingness to open up without discrimination to all of life's experiences, not seeing any difference in the four postures. This can be a bit difficult for absolute beginners when they come to meditate, because they haven't yet been able to access their undisturbed natural awareness through returning the mind to that natural stillness. A skilful way to address this can be by working first with a standard concentration practice, such as mindfulness of breathing. This is a particularly skilful practice to pursue because of its non-conceptual nature. If mindfulness of breathing is developed through concentration on the rise and fall of the abdomen, it will help to familiarize the practitioner with coming back into the body. This is a crucial feature of pure awareness practice and reintegration.

Q33. *Your site is really a wonderful resource, especially this forum. I have a question regarding insight practice within the general 'just sitting' or 'open awareness' approach to meditation. (My understanding being that 'pure awareness' is not something that can be described as a practice really, as there is no 'doer', but rather as the potential fruit of learning to contain and transform our emotional energies, or life force, as you call it, via opening to them without grasping or rejecting.) My question stems from something you mentioned regarding the ability of insight practices to severely* *undermine our basic sense of duality, of me here and the world out there. You say for example that the realization of selflessness, anatta, (along with the other two 'marks' of conditioned existence, dukkha and anicca) won't come about except as the result of implementing one or another of the insight 'tools' intended for burrowing deeply into the knots of our experience. This is clearly an intentional and therefore 'willed' practice, and I'm wondering if you could describe the most appropriate approach within the 'open awareness' method which you advocate toward cultivating insight (without, presumably, resorting to a more formalized approach). I guess my question hinges upon a bit of confusion relative to the basic 'not-doing' of the open awareness approach, as opposed to the more obviously deliberate approach of any of the insight practices I've been exposed to. I want very much to stick with the open awareness practice as I've understood it thus far, so would appreciate anything you could say about this.*

A. 'Open awareness', I think, may be better described as something more akin to a 'spirit' rather than a 'method'. This to me is where the crucial difference lies between this approach to practice and a more formalized one, because it is a practice that doesn't have an 'object' (and therefore no 'subject') of practice. How do we describe this so-called 'spirit'?

It is a willingness to open up to and accept all situations that we experience throughout our everyday life, both during and outside our periods of sitting meditation. This acceptance is certainly not a passive one, but requires inner strength to work against our tendency to fall into old habitual and emotional reactions. To restrain these habitual impulses requires awareness, and, crucially, the spirit to practise through all situations without picking and choosing – carrying on and functioning in as normal a way as we can, so that those around us don't even know that we are 'practising'. There is nothing to do but respond to what is in front of us, without trying to possess, manipulate or react, which are our normal everyday ways of dealing with things and life in general. This is where we get the notion that there is no practice. This way of practice – if we genuinely take it to all our everyday experiences without picking and choosing which ones we want to apply it to – is immensely difficult.

The nature of this practice, like all Dharma practice, is that it will bring up karma from the depths of our being, often so strong, that being able to bring forth the spirit I talk about becomes impossible. Bearing with these 'blockages' is a part of what we do, so that in time they lose their strength and fade into the background, so they no longer possess us in the way they used to do.

If some things refuse to shift, despite persistent effort and doing your best, making practice difficult or even impossible, you may need to focus on the particular attachment that is giving you this difficulty and give it 'special treatment' in order to free the log jam. This is where the more traditional ways of practice can come to our aid.

In my own experience I found the marks of conditioned existence to be very helpful in 'loosening up' my blockages, to dramatic effect. Most of the traditional practices may be helpful. Metta may be used to overcome anger and ill will, for example. Or the very useful formless practices of mindfulness of breathing can be used for several hindrances. In fact, these practices of the breath can always be kept at hand anyway, to help us settle and bring forth our awareness during meditation.

So when do we employ one of these 'skilful means'? This is where your teacher comes in, because a pure awareness practice requires a teacher more than any other kind. They will suggest a particular practice and they will tell you how you need to practise with it in conjunction with the spirit of your open awareness (which will always be there as the supporting framework), and when to drop this 'expedient means' and return exclusively to the pure awareness practice. One point worth mentioning here is always to remember that before we return to our own intrinsic awareness, there is first a long path of insight to travel. Slowly we unpick the delusion of self, and therefore much insightful deliberation into our make-up is needed. I would go as far as to say that I doubt there is anyone that would be able to go through their practice without needing a helping hand, at some time or another, from one of the deeply profound tools of orthodox Buddhism. I may also venture to suggest that it is only when in the latter stages of the ten bhumis that 'just being' becomes truly possible.

But always remember the key is never to lose the open all-embracing spirit that will one day 'pull the rug' from under the spell of samsara.

Q34. *How does mindfulness relate to awareness? How do each relate to the practice of loving kindness?*

A. I have tried to highlight the differences between the two in my second book, *Dharma Mind Worldly Mind*, so reading that should give you a good picture of my understanding on this vital subject. As to the specific relationship to metta, in my view, the principles apply in the same way as for any other 'subject' that is in our presence.

Mindfulness is the deliberate bringing of our attention to the moment and skilfully keeping it there. With metta we do that during the metta meditation. For example, musing over words, pictures, feelings and emotions, all retained with mindfulness. When we have reached that degree of familiarity we can bring to bear these experiences in our daily life and our relationship with ourselves, others, and life in general. This 'skilful means' can only be retained and nurtured with mindfulness as it 'battles' with the restless mind and self-interest.

Mindfulness promotes a one-pointed mind; when we have this, the fundamentally pure and eternally bright jewel of awareness is freed from the veil of our emotions (which is intertwined with the chattering deluded mind) and shines forth. It is in these precious moments that we realize our fundamental humanness, and our unfettered heart can respond to circumstances without hindrance and bondage, and spontaneously care for and love all that lives.

Q35. *I've been practising pure awareness for the last few months, which by coincidence have also been a few quite emotionally turbulent months for me. At various times I have felt quite lonely, angry, upset, betrayed. All of which have had an influence on how I feel about life and work and relationships. I haven't exactly been a*

happy camper! Previously I would have used the metta bhavana
practice to work on these 'negative' mental states, attempting to
bring about an understanding perhaps as to why someone close may
have done something to me, or to simply 'upgrade' my own experi-
ence of myself. Or I may have engaged in some chanting to shift me
out of a particular gloomy mental state. However, if I understand
the spirit of the pure awareness practice, then availing oneself of
such practices as these, is not to be done. Am I correct? Can you pos-
sibly say some more about all of this?

A. To have a devotional practice that could include chanting is certainly 'allowed', and positively encouraged, in this
type of practice. Furthermore, it is not only a very skilful
way of nurturing a positive relationship with yourself but
even more crucially with your inner nature, which is
beyond the turmoil of any relationship.

An example of devotional practice could be, as I have
many times mentioned both in writing and when teaching,
to incorporate bowing into the practice, which could be
accompanied with words of supplication and surrender. I
would regard the act of bowing as puja, or devotion, and if
regularly accompanied by sutta chanting, so much the
better. Regular engagement with this activity will support
the spirit of giving up the self, bring us closer to our inner
nature, and help to 'soften' the heart that has become 'hard-
ened' by self-interest.

When we become more aware of our inner nature, we
will by definition be more balanced and therefore naturally
more positive about ourselves as well. By learning to surrender to our inner nature with a devotional practice we

will unload not only the self (and help bring the warmth of our heart into the practice, which is crucial), but also the negative emotions that are associated with it.

Q36. *Much of my dharma practice has involved a 'cultivation' approach, trying to increase skilful mental states and eradicate unskilful ones. In trying to do this I have sometimes experienced a kind of alienation or dukkha, which seems to arise from striving to change myself. In this respect I have found the more receptive approach of the pure awareness practice a kind of antidote to this; it's felt very healing and opened me up to some of the fear and restlessness behind my striving.*

I find both these approaches helpful at times, but have difficulty integrating them. They seem to be doing quite different things with the mind; one approach attempting to manipulate and change our state of consciousness and the other just knowing our experience without altering or manipulating it in any way. These practices seem to work in quite contrary ways. By cultivating, are we not reducing our capacity to accept our experience as it is? Would you recommend sticking to one approach, or do you have any advice on integrating them?

A. Certainly stick to one way. I personally would feel concern if I discovered I was pushing away a part of myself in favour of another. I would be cutting myself in two, and that would lead to inevitable alienation. How could it be any other way? Wanting to become this and no longer wanting to be that is a common theme with practitioners. If this were genuine Dharma practice, I think I would be off doing something else. It sounds a dangerous path to follow, and could never be integrated into the effort to embrace the totality of ourselves without discrimination, which is what characterizes pure awareness. The Hinayana path develops skilful ways of 'suspending' the more 'unwholesome' side of ourselves by learning to turn away from it whilst developing the more 'wholesome'. This path is not a path of open all-embracing non-discrimination like the Mahayana, but this narrower way isn't really a path of rejection either. And by the way, give up 'striving to change' yourself. You'll tire yourself out.

Meditation in the Body

Q37. *In* Dharma Mind Worldly Mind *you talk about the importance of being in the hara. I must say that I experience consciousness more in my head and in my heart, on a good day maybe down to the solar plexus. I don't think I get as far as the point below the navel. If I try it in meditation I can get a non-specific sense of widening and opening there, but not a particular sense of consciousness. Do you think consciousness will just drop there with practice? What kind of emotions is the hara the seat of?*

A. We experience consciousness in the head, and it's here for the most part we think we are, and therefore where we live. But when we move our consciousness into the body, it crosses an apparent boundary and becomes awareness, and it is here that we alight on the threshold of the Dharma. Awareness is linked with and indeed caught by consciousness, but if we stay with our awareness (which is especially possible in formal meditation), our imprisonment in the narrow confines of dualistic consciousness begins to dissolve. From this point we begin to enter a vast expanse that has no limits, is bound by no 'person'. When we enter this expanse we can use the insight tools offered by Buddhism, which if nurtured correctly will transform and break through the limits of the samsaric world (which consciousness supports) into the infinity of our original nature.

From what you say it seems a good idea to cultivate still more deeply your experience of that expanse (samadhi) over a period of time, and then to make good use of that precious emptiness, with guidance, and begin to familiarize yourself with an insight practice.

As to your second query, all emotions originate in the hara.

Q38. *For the last couple of years or so I have regularly been experiencing the sort of physical jolts and strong rushes of energy when reaching a certain 'trigger' level of stillness, that you say in your latest book you learned of with some alarm from various meditators that you have spoken to. The general approach that you have taken in both your books impresses and makes a great deal of sense to me, and so I have taken to heart your advice here and have tried to dwell more in my hara, both during the mindfulness of breathing and metta bhavana practices, and also during the rest of my time.*

This has brought greater stillness and calm, less physical turbulence, and just feels right. However, I am finding some difficulty in each practice, but particularly the mindfulness of breathing in the latter stages, when I move towards, or attempt to move towards, refining the object of attention. I find it difficult to know how to move towards one-pointed awareness of my breath at the tip of my nose whilst simultaneously maintaining and deepening my hara awareness. The metta practice does not present such an intractable problem, although again I have some difficulty being fully in my hara at the same time as cultivating ever deeper and stronger metta. Can you enlighten me as to what I am missing here, please?

A. A major feature of cultivating practice is one of familiarity. In this particular aspect of practice we need to cultivate the ability to return to our body over and over again. The most important time to practice coming back is during our daily life. Catching ourselves mentally wandering off and coming back into the form over and over again, and being wholehearted in what we happen to be engaged in doing. This takes great commitment and endurance but in time we start to become familiar with our new state of being. We know this is the true state of awareness to be in and so we just come back more and more until it becomes a habit. When this becomes something really familiar, we will take that familiarity to the cushion, so abiding more and more in the body during formal meditation. To think you can just do it by an act of will when it suits you won't work.

Q39. *After meditating exclusively in one position for a number of years (half lotus with hands in dhyana mudra), I have begun to experiment with small variations of that posture (either with hands loosely clasped or with hands on the knees). I find that this definitely seems to affect energy flow in the body – dhyana mudra is more tightly focused and disciplined with an emphasis on balance; hands loosely clasped is very relaxing, good when over-stressed but leads quickly to sleepiness; and with hands on the knees the concentration tends not to be as tight, but the heart is wide open and my ability to contain strong emotion is at its peak. I still tend to sit mostly with dhyana mudra, but use the other two hand positions judiciously. This seems to have the desired effect, but I do wonder if* *tinkering with posture could be just a symptom of restlessness in the practice, and if it might be better to have one position and stick to it. What do you think?*

A. The experience of different postures is something that I've not had, so there is little I can say about what is best. It would seem to make sense to suggest that you use the posture that you feel most comfortable with, however, you do have a good point about swapping and changing.

It could be said that the totality of Dharma practice is nothing more than the taming of restlessness. If we take this to heart it should make us wary of wanting to change aspects of practice – in this case the posture used in sitting meditation. It is interesting that the hands are often held quite differently from tradition to tradition and sometimes from teacher to teacher, with each telling us why they use their particular style and why it is the best. Very confusing. It would make sense to follow the method of your tradition, but if you are someone who isn't committed to a specific tradition you will have to make a choice.

Your awareness that changing around frequently could be just restlessness is well founded, and I'm delighted that you are concerned about this. Any sort of change can often bring a 'honeymoon' period because of the novelty of what you are doing. When this period goes into change there is the temptation to change again, and so it goes on. My understanding of Dharma is to stick with things and for the most part let change take place of itself, whatever the aspect of practice may be. Letting yourself use different hand positions runs the danger of opening the door to other things, the 'thin end of the wedge' syndrome. All I can say is that it is not normal to change hand position regularly, so I would say stay with the convention. Pick one and resist the urge to change.

Q40. *I have been meditating with my eyes open since December and I have found it very powerful. I have heard of the eyes as 'gates', and keeping them open is a good way to open up and experience a breadth of awareness. Do you have any comments on sitting with eyes open versus shut?*

A. In my view having the eyes half open is a superior way to meditate. We associate having our eyes closed with sleep, therefore when we close them to meditate that familiar association could well lead us to drop off. Meditating with the eyes half-open creates a new familiarity, one that we only associate with meditation. This association should be part of the commitment to being wholehearted when we go to our cushion. To have the eyes half-open requires awareness and a willingness to do so. This has the added advantage that we can check whilst meditating whether our head is straight, through being aware of the line of light (whether it is straight or at an angle). Because we are committed to having our eyes half-open, our awareness will be present in our eyes, thus making them a 'gate'. Ideally our eyes should roll back naturally after we have settled and begun to concentrate. So we then look at the back or our eyelids (with the eyelids still half-open). With this achieved, as we begin to cultivate our particular meditation subject, we can stay present with more stability,

Q41. *My day-to-day practice is mindfulness of the breath and body, with the attention placed on the hara. In addition, I try to keep my attention in my belly as I move about during the day – with, of course, varying degrees of success. For some reason, I have a slight but steady sensation just above the bridge of my nose, between my eyebrows. It feels as though it is just below the surface of my skin, but does not seem to respond to massage or any sort of physical manipulation. I've had this for about a year. It seems to be connected with meditation, as it first appeared last summer during a 10-day vipassana retreat, and seems to intensify somewhat when I am meditating more often. It is not painful, just a small sensation like static electricity, with a faint pulse. It is always there.*

A. This is a common experience and really should be nothing to worry about. It is about gathering energy from concentration that backs up in the psychic channels, due to impurities. It is an experience I am familiar with. If you continue to retain your awareness and emotional energy [see next answer] in the hara, and learn to live in your body, you will be keeping yourself in balance. This way it should not get worse as you learn to live with it.

Q42. *On a possibly related note, during meditation I often experience short energy bursts. They occur when I am well settled and concentrated, and able to settle the mind well into the body. They persist so long as I can maintain the particular subtlety of attention – usually just a few seconds, but they will occur again and again until the session ends or I become distracted. They are fairly neutral in feeling-tone, tending a little bit towards pleasurable. Sometimes they make my body twitch a little. When I was on retreat, they sometimes came in short, single bursts while I lay in bed meditating*

– to the point it felt like they might knock me off the bed! If I have had a lot of stress recently and I lie down or sit up with the intention to 'feel into' my physical sensations, they will come up quite spontaneously.

A. It is all about living in the body. You mention in the previous question that you try to retain your attention in the hara. Whilst retaining your awareness down there you should also be retaining your emotional responses which come from habits and conditioning, with the aid of that same awareness. By learning to bring this crucial aspect of practice into your daily experiences you will be promoting health and safety in your life, and also bringing stability to your meditation. This is very much to do with turning away from the chattering mind and its blinding consequences and becoming grounded in yourself. So that when you walk you know you are walking, when you stand you know you are standing. Your twitching suggests that it needs to be worked on, as it is indicating you have lots of errant energy. If you have a physical job, so much the better. If you don't, then find something to help that energy on its way. If it gets worse you may have to consider cutting back on meditation for a while (a good way to test your attachment to sitting), because you don't want it to cause physical complications, as it often does for those who insist that Dharma practice is about working everything out in the head.

Q43. *I wonder whether you can clarify for me what exactly is meant by the Buddha's teaching on 'knowing oneself in all postures'? For example, I can mentally know that I'm sitting. Or I can tune into my physical experience, such as the sensations of the con-*

tact between my body and the chair, sounds coming to me. Or I can 'go inside' and have an inner feeling experience of myself in the moment, which takes the focus away from my senses, but seems to highlight a living presence within my form.

A. To have awareness of yourself in the moment is, I believe, what is meant here. To be aware is not to discriminate, but just to know. Be alive to yourself through awareness whether you are walking, sitting, standing or lying down. Nothing special, just know. Not to be wandering off in thoughts and unaware of what you are doing. There is nothing to do – just being alive and knowing it.

Q44. *I have been trying to bring my awareness into my body more throughout the day. This has been the most challenging while at work. I currently work as a social worker, and my job involves quite a bit of writing, listening, talking and analysing. The practice of mindfulness is usually talked about more in relation to sweeping floors or washing dishes. I have found it extremely difficult to stay in my body during my work activities, which seem to take place more in my head. I can sometimes manage it, but it does seem to detract from what I am doing. For example while listening to someone speak, I realize I haven't really understood what they have said because I have been more focused on my internal experience. Is it actually possible to stay in the body in these kinds of activities and still do them effectively? Or does a deep practice of mindfulness require that we refrain from doing work that is dominated by these activities?*

A. To return our attention to the body is a skilful way of gathering the distracting mind through the loss of awareness during our daily (and meditation) life, so that we return ourselves to the wholeness of an integrated mind and body. From this place of being centred we are not then meant to keep our attention there, but rather allow our clean unsullied (pure) awareness to 'fill out' into whatever is in front of us and the general environment. This fulfils both awareness and mindfulness. We are mindful of our direct experience (and deal with it accordingly) while also being aware of our surrounding environment. This way the whole of ourselves is brought to life rather than just the mental, as can be the case if we are only interested in developing focused one-pointed mindfulness.

Q45. *In my meditation practice I am increasingly working on my mind through the body. I feel I have very much sort of groped my own way of doing this. During a long retreat I have recently completed I experienced quite strong twitching and what felt like bolts or twitches of energy release in different parts of my body, which I don't understand or particularly know what's the best way to work with. More lately I've been experiencing regular sorts of energy releases from what I can best describe as the tail bone area, which seem to arise when I get concentrated or feel a bit inspired during my yidam practice. Could you offer any guidance on how to work with this in meditation?*

A. This is an issue I've dealt with on several occasions answering forum questions [see above]. Bringing your attention to the body and the hara area not just in sitting meditation but also throughout your daily life will familiarize you with the true and complete practice of reintegrating mind and body, and it is most important to be aware of this. Returning that wandering and erratic energy back into the hara again and again, and doing it with awareness, will promote a balanced practice of Dharma and give you a healthy, balanced body and mind. I have met many 'victims' in my time around Buddhism, practitioners who either have no knowledge of this or think it isn't important enough. But to me this is the most crucial issue in practice. To ignore this understanding and stay stuck in unskilful unbalanced habits will only get you into trouble, which could be serious and endanger you both physically and emotionally.

Q46. *I've been practising pure awareness on the cushions every day for the last few months alongside metta bhavana and visualization practice. I find the practice is enriching and seems like a necessary addition to my spiritual life. I find your comments regarding the hara very helpful and much of the practice seems to be bringing awareness 'home' to the hara. At times the experience of doing this simple practice is very energizing, powerful and balancing. Sometimes I seem to be aware of my bodily energy in a very different, more alive way. Energy blockages in the neck, shoulders and heart areas start releasing. I find when this happens I want to bring my awareness to these areas to try and release the energies there, but then I remember that I need to bring my awareness 'home' to my hara. When I do that, the intensity of energy in the shoulders, neck or heart goes. I can feel a bit dull or disappointed as everything seems so ordinary again, and I wonder if I have missed an opportunity to integrate these energies, which are strong but not centred in the hara. Any comments would be appreciated.*

A. You generally cannot release energy by just giving it attention where it happens to be. The best way to work with these experiences is to go to the area with your awareness and 'drag' the energy down to the hara with your awareness. By doing this you are returning the wanderer to its home. Once it is there, keep it there, and in this place learn to abide and return throughout your day. In time you will be able to cultivate your meditation in this place as well. This is integrating. There is nothing for you to 'do'. Just be ordinary.

If you feel disappointed, I can only think that you must be expecting something. Maybe some sort of reward or insight? Learn not to go down that route, because I can guarantee you will always be disappointed. Just cultivate the meditation and practice in general without seeking reward; this is the Dharma Mind. Certainly, fruit will come from correct practice, but when it will come and in what form is something you will never be able to predict.

Q47. *In your books and on retreats you talk of learning to open up to and accept painful negative emotions in a non-judgmental way when they arise as being crucial to transformation in Dharma practice. In this way, you talk of these emotions gradually softening and burning out and of us gradually returning to the natural warmth of the heart, and ultimately our true nature. You also talk of simply containing these emotions and not meddling with or manipulating them when they arise. At the moment, when I meditate, I am experiencing a lot of frustration in the hara and abdominal area, which is sometimes quite painful, to be honest. In working with this, I'm not sure whether to get 'more intimate' with this frustration, which sometimes seems to lead to greater 'wrestling' with the frustration, or to detach and observe a little 'back' from the emotion and simply allow it to be with a 'sky-like' attitude – maybe this latter approach is not so effective as it is more dualistic (I am not fully at one with* *the painful emotion, and therefore less releasing of the emotion can take place). Is there a balance that practitioners must find for themselves?*

A. Yes, a balance is very important, especially if the experience in the hara is particularly strong. I would say that if you don't retain your attention on the hara you run the risk of the energy running away with you, possibly causing trouble. On the other hand, forcing yourself to stay there may not be skilful either. A middle way is always best. Be aware, and return to retain familiarity with what you are doing, but also live your life in a normal dualistic way, as you describe it. This way you allow the life-force to feed itself naturally into what you are doing and do its job of keeping you alive in a balanced and healthy way. After all, that is what we are trying to accomplish. The time that you can be most intimate with the energy is during sitting meditation. Learn to take your awareness there and, if you have a subject-meditation, cultivate it from that position. If your meditation is a formless one, then use this experience to centre and ground yourself and from there allow your awareness to 'fill out' and become brighter.

Habits and Attachments

Q48. *Is spiritual practice all to do with getting rid of the so-called 'self' that keeps us separate from all that is?*

A. Spiritual practice isn't about getting rid of the self, because there isn't one to get rid of. It's about transforming the habits that give rise to a sense of self. If you try to get rid of the self it will only come back. And besides, it may well be the self doing the 'getting rid of'! Transforming the unbalanced emotional drive, which creates the environment for the sense of self to arise and attach in the first place, is the way to settle the paradox of self – that creator of all the worlds. This is the way of Dharma practice.

Q49. *I wonder if you have anything to say on the subject of renunciation. I may be wrong, but it doesn't appear to get any direct mention in your first book (besides practice being all about letting go!) What is meant by renunciation in Dharma practice, and do we westerners face any particular challenges? Didn't the Buddha say that without renunciation progress along the path is unlikely? What do you think he meant by that?*

A. I think you have already discovered the meaning of re-nunciation – you noted letting go. Giving up worldly pos-sessions, shaving the head, putting on robes and living a simple and austere life is the first stage of renunciation that a newly-ordained monk commits himself to, but that is only the beginning. With the exterior renunciation in place he then starts to work on the renunciation of his inner 'posses-sions'. For example, his emotional attachment to likes and dislikes, his opinions of right and wrong, what should be and what shouldn't be, etc., all those attachments that give us so much of our powerful self–identity. That grasping that sets the wheel of karma and becoming in motion. This in-ner surrender of our emotional attachments and habits is the real renunciation, the real 'going forth', and is the trans-forming process that is the essence of maturing on the path. Without this there is no 'progress' – as some like to say. Whether you are ordained or not, the 'rules' for renuncia-tion are the same.

There are no particularly unique challenges that I can see for westerners, other than learning to work with a very heavy self-view that we all seem to have and too much choice of traditions, as noted previously.

Q50. *In your book* A Record of Awakening *you make the fol-lowing observation: 'It is now impossible under any circumstances to enter into mental conflict with myself' (p.55). Question: Would you agree that if we come to a place of honesty in ourselves we dis-cover a characteristic that seems to manifest endlessly, which is that when challenged we invariably justify our actions, our feelings, our opinions (especially our opinions). 'I am always in the right' seems* *to sum up this unspoken attitude of mind. To compound the problem, this cast of mind is obscured by the 'noble' response (when the heat is off) that I am not always in the right, which I offer condescendingly, so to speak. But again comes the challenge, and in my reaction to it I revert, as night follows day, to the former defensive position. It is like saying, 'There is nothing wrong with me!' Can you say further how you reconcile these seeming opposites?*

A. Here is a classic example of the ceaseless mental dialogue and conflict that we seem to find ourselves in. Our embattled mind split down the middle, engaging in this endless dualism. And despite our awareness of it and the obvious experience of dukkha that it brings, there seems precious little we can do about it. It stems from an ingrained mental habit born of the non-understanding of reality; in other words, we are trapped in a dualistic world that is created by our own ignorance. We create a world of opposites not just on the outside but on the inside as well. This dualistic world, at play with itself, is where the phenomenon of a self arises. With the inclusion of the self it then becomes a game of self-defence, self-promotion and justification – the self is always reaffirming itself, as its basic characteristic is one of insecurity and fear. How it reaffirms itself is of no consequence to the self, as feeling alive is all that matters to it. So, for example, hypocrisy, and the obvious conflict that comes from that, is a good platform for its survival. How we deal with this very basis of suffering is what complete Dharma practice is about.

Q51. *Since faith is necessarily defined as confidence in something that has not yet manifested, does it have a place in insight at all?*

Since insight is based upon staying with the reality of the present moment and not getting caught up in ideas of future possibilities ('attainments', 'goals', etc.), surely faith has no place, since it represents the gap between what is and what I think might happen (or is possible). My experience is that a sense of 'rightness' in what I am doing comes from experience and insight, and not contemplating what might be possible and how to get there with my intellect.

A. Faith isn't needed for the unfolding of a specific insightful knowledge, as these moments are at the end of the journey, so to speak. Faith is needed in order to arrive at those moments. To experience that level of insight we have first to work through our blinding thoughts that have their roots in our powerful emotional attachments, anchored in the sense of self. The transformation of those emotional forces is very arduous and at times frightening, and tests the resolve of even the most dedicated of practitioners. By definition we are always going into the unknown on our spiritual journey, so we can never know what awaits us. Faith then becomes the indispensable tool that supports us through those difficult yet essential times that we have to endure and 'stay with'.

Don't imagine that faith is just a mental acceptance of something not known. It is that, but more crucially, it inspires and encourages us to bear with, thus developing the inner strength that is essential on our spiritual journey. If there isn't faith somewhere in the background of our practice as a support, then the journey will become, sooner or later, impossible to continue.

Q52. *Living in a city environment where there seems to be a constant media and consumer stimulus towards dissatisfaction and craving, how can this be integrated into daily practice without us becoming overwhelmed and restless?*

A. Dealing with this experience is very much at the heart of practice in a non-monastic environment. If you are someone who considers your practice to be essentially a sitting meditation one, then you will soon come to see how difficult practice can be in the life most of us lay people lead. It is because of this that it is essential we learn to work with these difficult and strong forces. I cannot add much more on this specific subject than I have highlighted in my second book, *Dharma Mind Worldly Mind*, and therefore would refer you to that for my perspective on this issue.

Learning to live and practice in a city environment is essentially about commitment, guidance, sangha, and a willingness to open up to and bear with (contain) the powerful inner emotional forces that, through habit, get caught up in the incessant seductive stimuli of city life. I assure you it can be done.

Q53. *How do you practise with illness?*

A. If you have a short-term illness such as a cold or 'flu, it is probably rather futile to try and meditate if your condition doesn't allow you to breathe or sit properly. Practice just may not be possible because you feel so under the weather. What is the use of struggling just for the sake of it, or do you think that you should practise in all circumstances, whatever they may be? I think a temporary incapacity such as this could unwittingly be presenting you with the opportunity to see just how attached you are to your practice and likely thoughts of making 'progress'. I've met people who like to say (with some pride?) that they haven't missed a day's sitting for months or even years. Is it this that drives them? – not to break that record even when the body (and common sense) is telling them they should be resting and taking it easy when they feel ill. A short illness could well be a golden opportunity to display non-attachment to 'your' practice! Never lose sight of the fact that the practice of Dharma, which is a practice of learning to become unattached, can ironically become the firmest of attachments and possessions.

A more long-term illness or even physical disability will be quite different, as you will have to learn to work with circumstances. The human condition is quite a remarkable one as we are the most adaptable of all animals on Earth. We can live in the hottest and coldest climates, in any type of environment, and adapt to whatever type of food is available. And so it is with practice. To accept and work with wholehearted commitment with physical limitations, and, crucially, the mental relationship with those limitations, will I am sure bring abundant Dharmic fruit.

Q54. *From time to time one experiences inspiration and joy in the practice. How can one best keep that from becoming a hindrance later on, when the inspiration fades, but the memory of it (and attachment to the memory) does not? How can we come down gracefully?*

A. I'm not quite sure from your question if you are looking at an insightful experience or simple joy that can arise from concentrated practice and a happy heart. Maybe we can review them both, as mara in his or her lust for attachment isn't at all bothered what your experiences may be.

As time goes by we are quite likely to have experiences that are insightful, joyous and inspiring. These experiences can be very powerful and evoke strong emotions, but once they have passed we must then be very careful how we move forward. Try to see such experiences as fruit of right practice and confirmation that your faith in the Dharma is well founded, and use each experience as an inspiration and support to let go of even more cherished attachments, moving ever deeper into practice.

I have spoken to several people over these past three or four years who have had strong insightful moments, and many then get so emotionally attached that they become obsessed by the experience. There are no special rules to apply at these times. If your experience is genuine, then you have already learnt that Dharma practice is grounded in letting go of emotional attachments to experiences. Experiencing insightful, joyful and inspiring situations is no different from experiencing painful ones, even though on the face of it we may think so. We normally work on attachments to what we would consider unwholesome and unskilful, and may think attachment to insight, etc. is OK because these are not defilements. But attachment is attachment is attachment, and therefore should be seen as the same. Practise in the usual way, and be very aware that attachment to the fruits of practice is especially powerful, and if you are not careful it will stop the practice in its tracks as well as inflate the ego.

Q55. *Would you say that faith (sraddha) is, to some degree, an experience of pure awareness?*

A. I'm sure that we all would agree that awareness comes in countless degrees. All sentient beings surely have it to some extent, however faint. We humans are different though, because we make the profound leap from having awareness to having self-awareness – a unique characteristic that can unlock the door to eternal freedom. Unlike animals and other forms of life, forever trapped by their instincts and karmic outflows, we, having precious self-awareness, have the ability to resist our habits and change our karmic outflows. We possess the potential to break the wheel of becoming.

For us Dharma practitioners this deeply profound state of self-awareness is the centre of our practice. Through training, we 'polish' our self-awareness – it becomes brighter and brighter as we understand more deeply who and what we are, what makes us this way, and how we can change. Through commitment to practice our awareness becomes so shiny and bright and alert to the present moment, it eventually shakes itself free, letting go completely the mind-made world that hitherto created the suffering and the dullness that blinded it to the truth of life. This we call enlightenment or awakening.

On this journey of purification we employ many skilful means, one being the nurturing of faith. Faith brought into our awareness helps us to let go of our attachments, so that awareness can cleanse itself of the deluded mind still further. When finally our awareness is totally cleansed and freed, we

can say it is pure. In that pure awareness no thing whatsoever can abide, not even a Buddha – and certainly not faith.

Q56. *Rather than getting caught up and over-identifying (i.e.,
anxiety, obsessive thinking) with difficult emotions or feelings, my
tendency is more to push them down and suppress them, as a way of
'dealing' with them. Often this action seems to happen uncon-
sciously, the fullness of a particular difficult emotion is put out of
my conscious mind. It then may come up, say, when in a quiet moment or especially on retreat. One side effect of this seems to be
sloth, blocked energy, which then becomes freed when the emotion is
finally fully experienced. Do you have any advice on how I can
counter this tendency to push down, and sit more in the fire of my
experience, pleasant or unpleasant, fully experiencing it when it
arises?*

A. We push these things away because we can't/don't want
to face up to what they are and the fear and self-loathing
that often results from them. To learn to open up to ourselves in a wholehearted and non-judgemental way is the
key to change, but it takes a lot of practice – and the key to
skilful practice is the understanding of the very important
concept of familiarity.

Familiarity means getting to know, over a good period of
time, our emotional reactions, and learning to resist the
temptation of falling into old and unskilful reactive habits.
Facing up to what we are is a very difficult matter, and,
when the experience is a powerful one, almost certainly impossible to pull off. So how do we go about dealing with
these deeply ingrained attachments?

We start with the small attachments that we have, which are (emotionally) manageable, and learn to contain and take them into the Dharmic environment. Here we can learn to look into them and understand how all these things become the sticky messes that they are. With this knowledge in place, it will allow us to contain the volition driven by the emotions so that the habit/fear and notions of 'me' can return to their original state before this 'pollution' took place – that is, Buddha nature.

Learning to work with the small things gives us that vital familiarity with practice; our fears then begin to ebb, giving us the courage to stay with other more difficult and traumatic experiences. Eventually we begin to see that actually there are no 'big' attachments to deal with at all, only an endless collection of little ones. As the old maxim states: 'Take care of the little things and the big things take care of themselves'. This familiarity and understanding gives us the courage to open up more and more and accept ourselves for what we are. Accepting ourselves without judgement leads us to loving ourselves, and in that spirit of love transformation of samsara takes place, allowing samsara to return to its original nature.

Q57. *Buddhist tradition uses several images of the need for single-minded determination in Dharma practice (I am thinking of the one in Zen of the sword about to rain down upon one's neck). Simultaneously, enlightenment is talked of as being always present, almost in quite an ordinary, simple, and easy way. Given that there must be value in both of these descriptions, how does one, or should one, apply effort in the spiritual life?*

A. Spiritual practice is always full of paradox. We must be wholehearted with total commitment, as if there were no tomorrow. And yet the fruit of such practice is to realize the everyday ordinariness of reality. As the famous Zen saying goes: How wonderful! How marvellous! I sweep leaves, I drink tea!

In order to realize what is in front of us, we need to apply single-minded determination, but single-minded determination in a correct way – a Dharmic way. This 'single-mindedness' should really be seen in inverted commas, for it can be misunderstood as ordinary worldly, wilful effort. Dharmic effort is the middle way, and this is different and very special.

Single-minded (Dharmic) determination is applied by not reacting in our familiar karma-producing habitual way to our everyday experiences, whether towards ourselves, others, or life in general. To, as it were, 'stand our ground' (emotionally) and through experience learn to create the Dharmic environment that transforms your attachments (not you), thus returning them to their original state. This requires a commitment so serious and immediate that we must accept the urgency to take this task in hand NOW, as it will be the only way to prevent our head being cut off and being forever lost in the death of samsara. To apply this immediacy we have to contain and just be our ordinary everyday selves, nothing at all special. When we are this un-fettered ordinariness, nothing special, then the middle way is attained and awakening takes place. We will return to the profound ordinariness of this moment.

Q58. *I wonder if you have anything at all to say about the importance, within the context of Dharma practice, of overcoming the tendency to either control or manipulate situations and/or people?*

A. For me your question gets right to the heart of what
Dharma practice reveals, which is our will to power. It's
what makes the world go around and is the reason for all the
suffering that exists. The will to power manifests most
clearly in our normal everyday life when we try to control
and even (sometimes very subtly) manipulate people or
situations (or both) for our own ends. This is the fundamental characteristic of the sense of self.

In practising the Dharma we are encouraged to look very
closely at ourselves to see who we really are, how we are put
together as a person. Thus we slowly come to understand
why we act in the way that we do. When we open honestly
to ourselves, we see there is nothing we do that doesn't have
something in it for us. More often than not, we come to see
that we do things so that they give us a sense of control over
our experience. It is as though we are always trying to be on
top and in control, for when we find ourselves not in control we feel vulnerable and fearful.

With this sense of self we create our sense of separateness.
Me here and the world out there. When we feel separate we
feel lonely and frightened, and as a result we need to take
control of life so as to avoid still more loneliness and fear. We
try to manipulate and control life, which in truth can never
be controlled and can never be the possession we crave it to
be.

Because your question gets right to the heart of our make-up, your query cannot be regarded as pointing at an aspect of our personality that we can target specifically and do something about. Rather, we need to see it as something that is addressed through the whole practice of Buddha-Dharma, whether ethics, mindfulness, understanding, or the complete opening up and giving of oneself to the refuges. Like any aspect of our make-up, if you feel that it gets out of control sometimes, bring forth the ethical side of practice through restraint with containment. But to transform satisfactorily our desire to control and manipulate, we need to practise the whole of the path with complete commitment and wholeheartedness.

Q59. *I am finding my working environment very stressful. I feel that I am working within a culture of blame and the work is often dissatisfying. While my work has an altruistic dimension to it, it often feels lost, mainly in anxiety. I have only been doing the job a few months. I have been reflecting on whether I am providing myself with conditions which are undermining my Dharma practice and am considering looking for something else. However, I have found your advice on 'sticking with it' helpful in other areas of my life, and am wondering whether the job actually provides valuable opportunities for working with strong emotions, like my desire to be liked and avoid blame.*

You have mentioned before your own difficult experiences of working in challenging work situations. My question is: How do you know when to stay with difficult conditions, as they may provide a valuable opportunity to 'stick with it', or when we should just leave them and give ourselves the help of a more 'supportive' environment?

A. This is often a difficult experience to call. As a general rule I would say, first, don't ever intentionally change your circumstances whilst in an emotional state; and, second, don't just compulsively walk out. Rather stay and bear with what you consider to be an unpleasant situation, and reflect.

Your situation could be judged to be a bad one for practice (many are), but this is often difficult to see clearly. We generally find it easy to convince ourselves that the situation we are in, and don't like, must be wrong for us! Let things run for a good while; examine yourself to see if this is a situation that you have been in before, one in which you may be experiencing that familiar demon of restlessness and want to run away. Or perhaps you are simply coming up against aspects of your personality that you find difficult to open up to.

If neither of these is true and your unhappiness doesn't shift, then look for another job. If after a while you find yourself feeling the same in the new job (because it is restlessness after all, or parts of yourself that you can't accept and open up to), then stay with this new job and learn to work with this powerful force of restlessness, and do your best to accept your limitations, learning to open up and bear with them while resisting the urge to try yet another work option.

Q60. *You often talk about working with strong negative habits, which may take years to soften and eventually break/transform. One of my own habits is finding porn on the net. Usually I 'go for*

*refuge' to porn when I don't want to engage with my own experi-
ence. Even though the experience of porn is quite unsatisfactory,
and I am aware of this to some degree, I often feel I can't resist the
pull, and soon find myself lost in this 'hungry-ghost' realm. Usually after a few days of 'escaping' in such a way I eventually get sick
and frustrated with it all (and also quite angry with myself).
Finally I find the will and positivity to engage with those emotions
I've been avoiding – often fear and sadness.*

*At the moment I'm much more willing to engage with difficult
emotions, but I know it's not the last time I will use porn to escape.
How can I make friends with this side of myself and acknowledge
my current weaknesses, but also work to transform them at the same
time?*

A. You can start the transforming process right now by
learning to make friends with your habit. Making friends
means to accept yourself the way you are and not to fall into
negativity, reactivity and judgements. These all empower
the habit and make it stronger.

Accept that this is the way things are just now, this is what
you lose yourself in. It's just the way it is. However, as you are
practising the Dharma, you have now decided that it's time
to turn away from a habit that isn't conducive to what you
want to do and (un)become. First, learn to be aware of yourself when you succumb to this habit and be aware of all the
strong feelings of attachment that go with it; start to see
more clearly why you run to such activities in the first place.
This is just to know. It isn't to judge and create a world of
opinions around it, it is just to know. 'When you indulge in
porn, know you are indulging in porn'. Next, learn to be

kind to yourself because you are caught by something of great power. Certainly don't think that this particular habit is wrong and bad. Actually what you are doing is perfectly normal, but maybe it's something you would rather be not doing. Learn to become comfortable with what is a powerful habit. Develop awareness around the experience and learn acceptance around it. Finally, develop restraint when this habit comes to you, so that over time you slowly develop the ability to pull back from being caught and carried by your conditioning.

Q61. *I frequently have a dilemma as to how to work with the spaces in my life. During periods of spare time I often notice I want to pick up a book or watch a film, but I am aware that there is a lot of restlessness driving it. Sometimes I just sit with it and do nothing, but sooner or later I want to do something. Is it unrealistic to attempt to 'just be' in all the spaces of our day, or would you advise carrying out the activity but just attempting to remain mindful as we do it?*

I have heard it suggested that refining our activities may be useful in this regard. For example, if my restlessness urged me to watch an action movie, I could replace it with something like listening to classical music or doing some kind of artistic activity, with the aim of channelling it in a more skilful direction. Sometimes I have felt more nourished by doing this and at other times only more dukkha. I would be grateful for any reflections you may have on approaching activities in this way.

A. For most of us, doing nothing can be one of the most difficult things to pull off. We are profoundly conditioned beings, and the need to be always 'productive' is very ingrained conditioning – especially for us western people. Just to sit, just to be, can evoke all sorts of emotions. Try, as an experiment, to just do nothing, and experience the intense frustration that can arise. How interesting! Restlessness, in a very real sense, is all that Dharma practice is dealing with – learning to be just with whatever is in front of us at any given moment without trying to possess or manipulate or avoid.

Something is always there, trying to possess or avoid the moment, and that is our sense of self. If it doesn't exert itself, then the self becomes lost and frightened. Stay with that frustration and allow the emotional upheaval that arises to come up and burn itself out, for that is surely what will happen if we don't react and fall into an old habit, like filling the gap with some activity. This is the usual reaction we have in these situations. On a deeper level what happens when we are still is that we begin to come into contact with our unprotected sense of self and experience its true reality – darkness, loneliness and fear. This is why we can hardly ever be still, always on the move, always avoiding our existential reality. By remaining still and allowing that fear to burn itself out, change will occur – true change – Dharma change.

Dharma practice is about working with whatever life presents us with. Sometimes we are busy, sometimes we are not. Practice is not a process by which we create things to work with, as this would become another activity of the self. Having said that, dealing with our emotional reactions through our everyday experiences can at times be too much for us, so allowing ourselves diversions from time to time can be a necessary reality. But the key is to be aware that we are diverting, and why. That's all, there is nothing to act upon, just to know is enough.

If you like action movies, then that is OK. I don't think making yourself engage with something 'cultured' is necessarily a better thing to do. But if you feel that that may help temper your restlessness, then give it a go. If you find that you are forcing yourself into something that others tell you will make you more cultured, yet causes tension in you, drop it. More refined cultural activities may well have qualities that could be said to be more harmonious with the qualities needed in spiritual practice, but there is always the danger of trying to turn yourself into another person. If you try to do this, you may just be replacing one persona for another, and what a waste of time that would be! Whether you appreciate Mozart or prefer a good goal scored in the rough and tumble of an emotional football match makes not a jot of difference to the Dharma. Skilful practice is about knowing yourself in all situations – whatever they may be. The living Dharma supports all life and is not concerned with the cultural values created by society. Just be yourself, learn to live in harmony with yourself, and the Dharma will love and support you.

Q62. *Sometimes while practising mindfulness I can feel like I am quite disconnected from others or what I am doing; I feel like I am holding back in a kind of self-conscious way, guarded, not quite letting go or something. I have noticed this can be accompanied by a sort of tension or seriousness about the way I practice, and live life in* *general. Perhaps I need to let go a bit, be a little more playful, but I am not sure how to bring this about. I would value any reflections you may have on this kind of experience, or advice you may have on how I may need to work with this.*

A. I think this is a very good question, and a situation that most of us committed to the Dharma could honestly admit experiencing. We take ourselves far too seriously, and the ingrained self-view (that we must protect at all costs) is the reason for this. When we see this, we see how enveloped and imprisoned we are by this self-view.

I think one of the skilful ways to deal with this is not to be afraid to make mistakes, or to make a fool of yourself in other people's eyes. Be prepared to experiment. When you are about to fall into an old familiar reactive way of looking after your image of yourself – and therefore retreating to familiar and safe ground – don't go there. Take the opportunity to open and respond in a different way. Always experiment and be prepared to take a chance. This might bring up self-consciousness and fear. Open to it, but don't retreat. Your new and previously untried action may mess things up, or could even be something unskilful that you think others will react to, but don't worry. Play with it with honesty and be prepared to get it wrong. Who knows? You may get it right. And if you should feel foolish, open to that. Is it really that important? Or are we only concerned with playing it safe and protecting that self-image? I believe to take the opportunity to loosen ourselves up in any given situation by not hiding behind our defences is vital in developing our ability to respond correctly and spontaneously to life's challenges.

Q63. *Buddhism stresses impermanence. A fruit of practice seems to be that one sees this more and more clearly in one's life. At times this seems to be leading me into more nihilistic states of mind. Do you have any advice on how I can work or turn this around to something more healthy?*

A. To see impermanence is a great liberating experience because it encourages us to let go of our attachments. We hold on and grasp because we want things in a way that suits us, yet at the same time we know that whatever it is I'm holding on to will sooner or later go into change, bringing the inevitable grief of loss. When we finally accept the reality of impermanence and become not so caught up in our habits, we grasp less at things in our life, and begin to taste the spaciousness that letting go will bring.

Seeing impermanence more clearly can be experienced as being nihilistic because our lives are always about reaffirming the sense of self through attachment. Taking refuge in impermanence can bring emotional unease and fear at our growing loss of self-identity. In fact, what happens over time is we become a lot more content with the simplicity that comes from not chasing old habitual attachments and find ourselves opening up to new vistas in our life that bring us to greater fulfilment. Walking this path, like so much in the spiritual life, often requires us to put faith in the subtle way of genuine change and not be too hasty to fill those newly found spaces in our lives with still more things to do.

Q64. *Some time back I had a discussion with someone whom I would look to as having a strong connection with the Dharma. In the course of the conversation he spoke about the demands of true practice and the need to let go of egoist desires. When he said this I was taken over by a deep sense of sadness and grief almost. It was as if I had been told that my death was just around the corner and I was left with regret for all those things that I wished to do in life that I had never gotten to do. Honestly, I was almost depressed. In fact rather than being inspired to practice, I was more saddened about the passing of life. It really struck me how unwilling a large part of me is to truly let go of my own plans for my life. So I'm left wondering, whether in the absence of this basic (tough, deeply critical, challenging and key) requirement for the arising of insight, is there really any point in practising?*

A. Dharma practice is about letting go. Letting go of our desires and aversions driven by this sense of self. This is a lovely ideal, but when we come to put the theories into practice and begin to taste how practice works, then we can have a few shocks as to what we've let ourselves in for. Our life begins to change, and also the aspirations that we previously cherished. We discover that when we begin to let go of our attachment to our desires, those very desires often begin to fall away as well. We discover that those desires weren't for fulfilment in life, but were there for another reason, and that was solely to enhance the sense of self. Now we are learning to let go of the self, certain life aspirations, as we had thought of them, begin to recede into the background as well. This can result in a sense of fear and loss. 'What is life all about, if it isn't about pursuing what I want?' can be the cry. There will be emptiness and loneliness. To let go of self-motivating desires will be like dying, we will feel sad and desolate at our loss. But we learn to trust the Dharma, and stay with what is a basic existential experience. If we have faith and trust in the Dharma, through practice we begin to hand ourselves into that 'dying', to find a rebirth begins to take place. A rebirth that isn't driven by a sense of self, but a rebirth that is truly mysterious. It is mysterious because it is spacious and spontaneous, and beyond the cycle of birth and death. It is the true self, fearless and warm-hearted.

Q65. *In one of your talks, as an example of containing emotions, you talked about holding back from shouting at your housemate who had just used up all your milk, and instead, experiencing the strong emotions fully in the body. Is it not possible in such a situation to skilfully discuss the problem with your friend – perhaps later when the anger has gone? I have found this approach productive in my own experience, so long as it is done with kindness. Surely there is more to right speech than silence.*

A. I was referring to how to deal with the experience at the time, how we can send that habit of losing our temper into change through containing. You are absolutely correct to say come back to the experience with your friend and discuss the issue when the emotion has subsided. This way we are in a more rational, balanced human state, and it is from here we can skilfully deal with the situation.

The Diverse Fruits of Practice

(Q1.) [This is a repetition of the opening question in Section 1, for the reason given in the Editor's Note.] *I have attended some Sunday practice days and a week-long retreat with you, but I am still unsure as to what practical aspects of meditation you are teaching. Are you teaching the noble eightfold path, four noble truths, etc., as the means to liberation, or a combination of the different traditions you have practised in? For example, your website talks a lot of 'pure awareness', but my understanding of the Buddha's teaching is that meditation practice and insight are cultivated by the eightfold path, i.e., establishing oneself in the precepts, developing awareness and concentration initially by breath awareness and then by mindfulness of the four elements of experience taught in the* Satipatthana Sutta, *while developing right thought and right view with an aim of developing equanimity (with the awareness) through the insight of impermanence, unsatisfactoriness and non-self? Could you explain how similar your teaching is to the many vipassana traditions practising from the suttas, with their emphasis on both awareness and equanimity (and thus right view) as the means to liberation?*

A. Your question outlines the conventional so-called developmental path, whereby all the features you describe are highlighted and cultivated. This as we all know is revealed most clearly and directly in the Pali Canon. The Canon is the bedrock of orthodox Buddhism, and is practised and taught to this day by the Theravada tradition. But there is a second way. Without getting involved with the controversies that surround this alternative way, it is in fact the bedrock of Zen, and is the pinnacle of the manifold practices of Tibetan Buddhism and is known as Dzogchen. The teaching of the so-called sudden path (such a misleading and misunderstood name, for it invariably take years of committed practice to arrive at this 'sudden' awakening!) also go back to the beginning of Buddhism, but these teachings are barely touched upon in the Canon.

Rather than cultivate one by one the numerous skilful means on offer with the highly conceptualized gradual path, the sudden path, so to speak, 'leaps' over them all and positions itself at the door of awakening – the same door that the developmental path will lead you to, because there is only one path and one door to awakening.

It is crucial here to accept that each of us has Buddha nature, and therefore we all possess the innate qualities of awakening. If we can accept this, then we have the starting point, from which all we then need to do is wake up to what we really are. I don't want to get into a long description to validate this form of practice, but I do want to emphasize that to awaken to our true nature we need only to learn how to drop the veil that is separating us from it.

We learn through deepening wisdom (non-attachment) over many years to let go of that veil, which is nothing other than a collection of habits built up and embraced by that phenomenon called 'self'. This letting go is done through uncluttered awareness, slowly becoming awake to the stillness, spaciousness and brightness of just seeing. Such experience is to taste our true nature. We then learn to abide in this profound state still more, in that bare open experience of our true nature. This is not at all easy. We need support and guidance to become more familiar with this profound state. It is the state that leads us to the direct uprooting of our dualistic mind and liberation through awakening.

If we look very carefully at this practice, we will discover all the features that you describe above. To give you just one example: the stillness that reflects your natural unborn stillness is only possible because of – even if only for a short time – 'practising' ethics, concentration, and wisdom – i.e., the eightfold path. When your mind is still, open and receptive, are your ethics not perfectly in place? Is your concentration not perfectly in place also? Without long training and learning to let go of the world that we are normally caught up in, how would it be possible to have this ability to be still? So is it not the presence of wisdom (non-attachment) that is making this experience possible? Here is the direct experience (like the analogy of the ice cream described elsewhere). It is the direct experience of the moment before thinking, before even the conceptual formula of the eightfold path comes into being. Look at this experience closely. Before conceptualization, all eight steps of the path can be seen, not just on their own, but each step supporting all the others. Each step is seen to be actually penetrating each of the others, thus becoming the one direct living experience, before that concept of the 'eightfold path' arises. The eightfold path is said to be the fourth noble truth, but actually the middle way is the true meaning of the fourth truth. The middle way is not a formula, but the direct experience of going beyond the pull of the dualistic world and living in the now. And living in the now is when you directly experience the taste of the ice cream, before the world arises.

The two ways of sudden and gradual can so easily be seen to be so far apart that many are sceptical they are the same path. But on closer examination we see they are not two at all, but rather two different ways (that suit different temperaments) along the same ancient path leading to the same ancient city.

Q66. *What advice would you give on practising with doubt? How should one set about cultivating confidence in oneself and faith in the Dharma?*

A. Doubt can only successfully be settled by practice. Take on a complete practice and learn to work with mental and emotional doubt, that is, don't be pulled around by those negative thoughts, but learn to stay with and contain them. Learn to carry around with you the emotional impact that doubt creates in the depths of your body, as you cultivate practice. Conviction will come from the fruit of practice; confidence in yourself and the practice will naturally follow.

Don't fall into the trap of thinking all you need do is read just one more book (or two) to rid yourself of doubt.

Faith will help disperse doubt, but always remember true faith comes from experiencing the practice and its fruit. So rather than having faith dependent on others, do the practice!

Q67. *Sometimes one hears of Dharma practice spoken about in terms of growth and development. Is this a valid way of approaching practice? Is there a danger of a western preoccupation with the self and ego leading to a wrong take on practice?*

A. When we correctly practice the eightfold path embraced by going for refuge, 'growth and development' will unfold naturally as the fruit of practice. If we try to shape it, and make it how we think growth and development should be (or rather, how we would like it to be), then you can be sure this will become delicious fodder for the self as it proceeds to reshape itself into becoming a wonderfully wise 'enlightened being'.

Q68. *Is it important to get the self into some sort of shape before true practice can be undertaken?*

A. It is true we need to have a fairly good relationship with ourselves in order to cultivate the path. Learning (maybe with a particular meditation developed for this purpose, such as one of the Brahma Viharas) to make friends with ourselves (and others) at the beginning of practice does help. But do see it as a useful tool that you use by choice rather than considering it to be something that must be done as the beginning of your practice. As the whole of authentic practice of the Dharma, even in the infancy of day one, is nothing more than an ongoing deepening process of making friends with ourselves through the cultivation of wisdom, we will be engaging in true practice anyway.

Q69. *If I understand you correctly, (loosely speaking) you define right livelihood as being that which is supportive of one's practice, a livelihood that doesn't consume all of one's time and energy leaving one with little space for being with oneself and practising. Should right livelihood also have an altruistic dimension, so that one may 'serve the Dharma', as it were?*

A. I would say that right livelihood is a livelihood that is sympathetic to observing the precepts and developing ethics. As far as having time and space in your life is concerned, this is more to do with your ability to take control of your life rather than being its victim, and does not necessarily relate to right livelihood. If you practise the Dharma correctly all your actions serve the Dharma.

Q70. *I was reading the forum and noticed in answer to a question about right livelihood you make the statement: If you practise the Dharma correctly, all your actions serve the Dharma. I found this statement really powerful – could you maybe say more about this and how to orientate oneself in this direction? How does one learn to live in this way?*

A. We should not be deceived by appearances. Because someone is engaging themselves in, for example, Buddhist activities of various sorts, doesn't by definition mean they are practising the Dharma. The motive to help others selflessly could be well down their list of priorities. Their primary motive could be promoting their own self-image through being respected, being well thought of. What they are doing could well be useful and beneficial to others, but in practice terms it will have a superficial impact on their transforming process, which is what Dharma practice is about. Indeed, they could be just pumping up their ego still further.

In strict Dharma terms what you do on the outside (providing you observe the precepts) is of little consequence to the cultivation of the path. Of course some activities are more conducive to practice than others, but broadly speaking it doesn't matter what you are doing. To put a correct practice in place is the first priority. That correctness is centred on understanding the eightfold path, a path laid out to enable you to come back with mindfulness and awareness to whatever you are doing, and to stay centred. When you are centred there is no sense of a self; it is here that selflessness abides. Whatever action you now do is non-karmic producing and deeply profound. Here you are not only honouring and serving the Dharma (indeed, you are the Dharma) for your own benefit, but also honouring and serving the Dharma for others around you who are bound to be touched by your obvious selflessness, and inspiring them to practice.

You learn to orientate to and live the Dharma by learning and putting into practice the eightfold path supported by going for refuge. This is the framework of the path (irrespective of the tradition or method you follow). You get your guidance from your teacher and from moderate study, all within the support of a sangha. It is a long and steady process that you surrender your life to in the spirit and determination of a full-time commitment.

Q71. *Lately I seem to keep meeting with 'healers' and having conversations about healing with them. So much so that I'm wondering whether there might be some meaning to all of this for what I should be doing with my life. At least in the short term? Do you think that the Dharma interacts with each of us in our daily lives, and through chance meetings, conversations, etc., gives us clues as to what we should be doing in order to have a more effective practice and to make progress? I guess a more broad way of putting this question is: If one reaches toward the Dharma, does it respond in kind and interact with one's life? If so, how does one go about identifying what is Dharma interaction and what is just 'pie in the sky'?*

A. The restless mind and wishful thinking is usually the architect of 'Dharmic omens'. Keep your feet on the ground and deal with what is in front of you. When genuine change is about to come to you, it usually becomes clear after you give the possible new situation space (and time) within yourself. Then you will see the next thing to do, clearly. NEVER be impulsive.

One reaches towards the Dharma, as you put it, by practising the eightfold path, embraced by going for refuge. If you do this, then you will have your feet firmly on the ground and be less inclined to be looking for signs and omens to rescue you from your restlessness and dukkha.

Q72. *I have a further question that has arisen having read your book. In relation to the bodhisattva path you mentioned that dwelling on wisdom whilst meditating can help to deepen one's practice. Do you liken this to dwelling on the 'appreciation' of higher spiritual states and values? I would very much like to hear your views on this subject and what your recommendations would be to cultivate this wisdom in one's practice.*

A. The reference in the book (*Dharma Mind Worldly Mind*) to dwelling on wisdom refers to it as a 'skilful means' to recall your own insightful understanding, which can help deepen still further your concentration during meditation, not others' understanding that you may have read about or heard. My recommendation, as ever, is to commit yourself wholeheartedly to cultivating the eightfold path embraced by going for refuge. If you pursue the path in the correct way, the values and qualities you mention will slowly mature within your own heart, and become self-evident. If it helps you, you can study books and then ponder these characteristics and qualities to orientate yourself in the Dharma, but be careful not to turn yourself into a parrot and merely think about and recite what you have read or heard.

Q73. *After studying an introductory course at the London Buddhist Centre last year, I had some strong opposition to it from my partner. Although I made it clear that I wasn't about to take up the robes and leave her (!), but that it would continue to be part of my life, I have, intentionally or not, become somewhat of a closet follower of the Dharma. Should I be concerned about this?*

A. No, not at all. 'Coming out' can be very difficult and often takes quite a long time. Be in no hurry, and trust in what you are doing. Confidence will grow and you will naturally become yourself. It's easy to imagine that because others have little or no knowledge of Buddhism, somehow they will become suspicious of you. Indeed, that may well happen. Let those around you slowly get used to your new interest. Often they may feel threatened by what you are doing, and if it's a partner that feels uneasy, it may be that they are concerned that you may change and leave them. Give these important changes in your life time to settle and become familiar to those around you, communicate with them and let them see that you are not starting to grow horns or are about to do something silly.

Q74. *Could you talk about the correct way to practice humility? Sometimes I think we westerners can confuse it with feelings of servitude or guilt, especially if we have a strongly theistic religious background.*

A. Cultivating humility is something that westerners need to be careful with, as it is something that doesn't come easily to us. If we 'try' to be humble, we enter the danger zone. Who is it that wants to be humble anyway? We could so easily become one of those self-righteous, not to mention judgemental, types of people, ending up with an even bigger ego. So how do we bring this essential quality into our practice?

Humility is that quality that begins to grow of itself through time in practice. Our willingness to contain our habitual outflows and not to go down the familiar road of reactivity is to deny the self, to deny its desire to reinforce itself and to be in control. This containment is the actual surrender of self; so the turning away from the self's desire for fulfilment in this way naturally becomes the cultivation of humility. Not as something you do, but the natural consequence of not bringing the grasping nature of self to whatever the situation may be. By practising in this way we slowly begin to become familiar with the experience of not wanting to have things our way all the time. And we begin to waken up to the reality that not wanting things our way actually begins to open up a freedom of being that can genuinely change our lives.

To encourage the development of this quality still further, I've discovered that the act of bowing can be of profound support. Humility is to accept that there is something far greater that is beyond 'me', my possessions and my desire to control. Whilst bowing in front of a Buddha rupa, in your mind gather up all possessions and notions of self and hand them to the Buddha. All of them, including those possessions that you regard as spiritual insight and wisdom. Unload yourself of everything and ask the Buddha to help you to give up all of these sticky possessions. In that emptying, there will not be the void that you may imagine, but the warmth of humility when you realize that beyond the blindness of self, a vista of something profound and far greater than 'me' opens up. Oh, and don't forget also to hand over the one that is doing the handing over!

Q75. *I have heard it said that it is possible for a person to attain stream-entry without realizing it has happened to them because it* *has happened very gradually over many years of practice. Do you think this is true?*

A. The breakthrough is always sudden, irrespective of the tradition or particular way of practice. Preceding the break-through there is an accumulation of (worldly) wisdom, which leads us to the ability to let go of our habits and attachments. When letting go has matured sufficiently, the middle way (fourth noble truth) is perfected, that is, in the worldly context of the middle way. With that, the 'carpet' is pulled unexpectedly and suddenly from under the dualistic samsaric world, which then collapses, and awakening takes place. If this is not obvious to the Dharma-farer, then they need to seek out their teacher to clarify the experience. If it is obvious to the Dharma-farer, then they still need to seek out their teacher, to get guidance and support in letting go of the attachment to awakening...

Buddha Nature

Q76. *You say in response to a forum question [below]: 'True emptiness expresses itself through the warmth of the human heart, which when truly liberated is all that is.' Later, to another question [also below], you say: 'The deepest meaning of emptiness is interpenetration, and it is because of this truth that all designations are false, yet there is always love.'*

I was very struck by both statements, just as I have always been struck by the undeniable fact that in all the thousands of years of cruelty and warfare, love has never been 'conquered'. Amid all the horror, we still care for and reach out to one another, which is both remarkable and inspirational. Is there a connection between your statements and my observation? I wonder if you'd care to comment further?

A. The answer to this question can be found in these observations. Buddhism characterizes our everyday dualistic mind as having greed, aversion and delusion, created by the sense of the all-grasping self that constantly reaffirms itself through actions based on these characteristics. Love, on the other hand, is the natural condition of reality, of our true nature. Reality is sometimes described as emptiness (shunyata).

The sense of self must appropriate what comes into its experience. Love on the other hand, being the natural condition of our true nature, is in itself impersonal, pervading and supporting all of life – yet through sentient beings love expresses itself. Because our true nature is ever present love is ever present, therefore always available to the self to appropriate. This it tries to do, always trying to make it 'me and mine'; selfless natural love can then appear to become tainted with self-interest.

Paradoxically, beyond the clutches of that possession-of-the-self called 'love', real love is never actually touched and remains always present, because real love is the nature of shunyata, with compassion as its expression. Everyone's true nature is love. That is why true love is always beyond our created dualistic world-version of love and therefore indestructible.

Without love, life for us would not be possible. With greed, aversion and delusion as its armour, the sense of self is always trying to possess the experience of life, thus creating the imbalance that we all experience and call unsatisfactoriness. Yet life is always in balance because love is always there as the counterbalance, and always breaking through the human condition to express itself through compassion. Because true love is always present, that counterbalance will always allow us to rebuild after our desire to destroy has run its course. Love will rise from the ashes and rebuild life, because love is life itself and so powerful it could never be defeated. As long as there is life there will be love. And even when all life has gone, love will still be...

Q77. *In a recent posting to the DharmaMind forum, you mention that Dharma is a mysterious movement of the living Buddha, and something we should learn to open up to and become intimate with. Elsewhere, I've heard teachers talk of opening to 'other power'. In your book* A Record of Awakening, *you speak of being guided and supported by the Buddha. I wonder how we can develop a sensitivity to the movement of the living Buddha in our own lives, how do we cultivate and deepen this important relationship, and how can we identify it at work? What is its nature?*

A. We develop our relationship with our inner nature (other power, perhaps) through commitment to the eight-fold path. This is embraced by going for refuge – in other words, by practising the Dharma. To answer your question more precisely, we need to focus more on the refuges, in this case, the Buddha refuge. The refuges represent more the spirit of, and commitment to practice. We need to be willing to open up to our inner nature (Buddha), learning to nurture a relationship, through commitment and familiarity, that will allow us to let go of our precious attachments. Attachments in which we invest so much of the sense of 'me'.

As we live in our heads, blinded by the sense of self, we are for the most part estranged from our original nature. Separate and isolated from the whole, we live lonely and frightened. We need to learn to trust that which is beyond 'me' and become sensitive to the truth that we are part of an inseparable whole that is forever in a state of flux. We need to turn our attention to that which lives 'behind' the self, learning through practice to hand that sense of self back to its original nature.

That sense of self has habits driven by the emotions. We are learning to contain them through practice, but we have the greatest difficulty doing this. By turning inwards and opening up to ourselves through containment we can hand that habit to the Buddha.

Cultivate the practice of bowing, and with your awareness focused inward ask him to help you with your burden. Admit you cannot contain this emotion on your own. You so much want to give this sense of self away and be free from its eternal bondage, but you cannot do it on your own. Bow down to the Buddha and ask him with the utmost humility to help you. Disarm yourself of your defences and conceit and ask him to support you in your time of need. Does this sound a bit God-like and Christian? The Buddha is not 'out there', nor has he created you, nor is he a separate entity that comes to your aid, but your true nature, which you live out of second by second, and have done so since time began. He is eternity, everything, and beyond comprehension. But because his nature is one of wisdom and compassionate warmth, he 'brings himself down' to your level so that you can comprehend and communicate with him. Learn to trust and over and over again, through containment and bowing, hand that precious 'me' back. Back into the inconceivable warmth and love that yearns to help you. So that one day you will return and re-unite with the wonder of the Buddha, and your true home.

Q78. *Is it possible when doing this practice of pure awareness that one could get it all wrong and reduce Buddha nature to simply the experience of sense-based phenomena? Surely Buddha nature is far more than just this mindfulness of the world of the senses!*

A. Whilst at times it may be easier to say 'the practice of pure awareness', it is not actually possible to practise pure awareness. This is just another paradox that characterizes so much of the spiritual path. Conventional language is often easier to use to put the point across, but practice is what actually takes you to its threshold. Awakening to pure awareness is the fruit of practice. It is not possible to get Buddha nature wrong, as you put it, because there is no Buddha nature to get wrong. In order to awaken to Buddha nature it is necessary that we train in and cultivate the right spirit of practice. This spirit is not a formula or anything that can be worked out. Rather, it is an attitude of opening up to something that is beyond 'me'. This needs a spirit of surrender to be nurtured, a spirit that is, in my view, the true meaning of going for refuge to the Buddha, Dharma, and Sangha. Because of emptiness, Buddha nature is all that is, both samsara and nirvana, yet also neither. The deepest meaning of emptiness is interpenetration, and it is because of this truth that all designations are false, yet there is always love.

It is very easy for us to get lost in notions we have about practice somehow reducing reality – in this case termed Buddha nature – to something akin to a formula or a metaphysical construction. We ought at times to remind ourselves that Buddha nature would best be thought of as being alive, wise, warm and compassionate towards all living things, and with love for all that is. The all-embracing ever-present truth.

Q79. *How does Buddha nature arise? Could one say that it springs forth from emptiness?*
A. I would say Buddha nature arises from wholehearted practice, and springs forth from commitment. When you apply yourself to wholehearted practice, practice that you are prepared to take into the whole of your life in a consistent way, then you enter the transforming process that Dharma practice promises. If you stay with your practice and continue with this same commitment, one day your true nature will open in front of you, and all the questions that you have ever asked or pondered will be answered.

Q80. *Lately I've been reading material by certain contemporary teachers (not associated with any particular religious tradition) who claim to have had 'awakening' experiences. They seem to suggest that 'consciousness' doesn't care about any single individual's needs, spiritual or otherwise. I may be incorrect, but I think I recall you saying similar at one of your talks. You said something to the effect that the Dharma doesn't care what any one person is looking for from their spiritual life. However, you also seem to suggest that consciousness does indeed respond to a seeker's need for assistance. You speak of bowing to this consciousness/divine, of asking for help and direction. From my own experience, there does seem to exist a dynamic, or an interaction between something in myself and something beyond me. But I wonder whether out of a deep need for security I am simply fooling myself! In an infinite universe, why should consciousness care about me! Do you know what I'm* *getting at? I wonder whether you might be able to say anything about all of this?*

A. I find your question somewhat confusing but I will do my best to comment. First of all, I'm not sure what you mean by 'consciousness'. Let's assume you mean that which Buddhists refer to as Buddha nature (or sometimes referred to as original or true nature). Yes, I have said that Buddha nature isn't interested in how you want practice to be, whether you want to have it on your terms, or at your convenience. Our true nature will respond when we learn to practise correctly, having the humility to surrender ourselves throughout all our everyday experiences of life, not picking and choosing the ones to open up to.

It is possible to cultivate communion between yourself and Buddha nature, but never imagine Buddha nature to be 'out there'. It is your true nature and is within you. Yes, you can fool yourself, thinking you are communicating with Buddha nature when in fact it is your deluded mind playing games.

Communion can only take place over time, through cultivating wholehearted practice, practice in which you are prepared to engage yourself full-time, in all situations, and learn through humility to give yourself up. Give yourself up to what? Give yourself up to your true nature, that which is within all of us. If you call upon help only when it suits you, and consider it something of a convenience that will get you out of trouble, then this is an example of your delusion. There is a price to pay for the wholehearted relationship, and this is the surrendering of the self. If you want this relationship at your convenience, then it will never happen, you will be forever drawn into the deluded self's desire to have things on its terms.

Your true nature loves you as it loves all beings, and indeed all of life. It 'aches' to reach out and help because it cannot be any other way. It sees you not as something separate but as itself, as nothing is separate, but at one with Buddha nature. There are not many Buddha natures; this only appears to be so because of our inability to grasp the all-embracing reality of one Buddha nature – the great eternal mystery that is never touched by time and space that is the wisdom that is not separate from love. And because it cannot be known or grasped, our response can only be to bow our heads with humility.

Q81. *Is awakening 'an act of grace' (or words to that effect) or is it a reward for effort on the part of the spiritual seeker? Isn't the very notion of a spiritual path self-defeating because it does the one thing that has to be undone? Namely, by focusing attention on something to be achieved in the future, a goal to be attained, etc., it traps the seeker of nirvana into a time-line? All this doing and striving-after that spiritual practitioners get up to, isn't it all just more stuff for the 'self' to be getting caught up in, more fuel for its unending need to create itself?*

A. I'm not sure what you mean by 'grace'. If you mean that someone or something gives you a prize for your efforts, well, I don't think so. Our part on the spiritual path is to learn, through making use of the tools of practice, how to give ourselves up, surrendering the notion of self that attaches and creates life's problems. The 'reward', as you put it, is the natural fruit of practice that falls when the conditions are right, returning 'us' to our own eternal true nature, which is warm and loves all that is.

There is a timeless paradox within spiritual practice. Commitment to a spiritual path invariably means making use of supports and systems, including religions. In Buddhism we refer to these as 'the raft'. The raft ferries us to the 'other shore', and once there we let go of the raft. For most of us, to get to the other shore on our own, without support and guidance, would be impossible. The Buddha (like all great spiritual teachers) recognized this reality and created supports to help us in our commitment.

We call it the 'Buddha-Dharma' or 'Buddhism'. There are those that say that such things create attachment and a sense of doing something, of trying to go somewhere, and trying to become something, and therefore can never work. This is true if you don't know that what you are making use of is merely a 'skilful means', something to let go of when it has fulfilled its purpose. This includes the whole network of supports and teachings that collectively is known as 'Buddhism'.

You may well imagine that when the moment arrives to return to your true nature after many years of cultivating Buddhist insight, you will be full of wisdom. This notion couldn't be further from the truth. When the moment arrives for you to return to your true nature you are no longer a 'Buddhist' or any sort of conditioned being. Even the wisdom that has brought you to this moment deserts you. Rather, you are like a newborn baby that knows nothing and is incapable of any attachment.

If you decide that you don't need a raft of any kind, then be aware that this way of practice can be fraught with dangers. What we are engaging ourselves in is indescribably subtle. If you feel that you are someone special, not needing to make use of the checks and balances that all the great sages have made use of throughout the ages, then be careful. You run the grave risk of straying up a blind alley, all the while convinced you've got everything right.

Q82. *At the end of your second book you describe your practice of bowing. You say: 'On the first bow I quietly ask the Buddha to forgive me.' I find it easier to cultivate a 'confession of faults' attitude than one of asking for forgiveness. It seems a bit Christian to me. Who or what is doing the forgiving? Is it that ultimately only something deep within myself that can forgive all my own faults and mistakes?*

A. Who or what would you confess your faults to? Yes, it is ultimately only something deep within ourselves that can do the forgiving: Our own true inner nature. The nature that is eternal is the great mystery that embraces all of life. It is that which we live out of every second of our lives, yet it is forever beyond the entangled world that we are familiar with. It is this that I personally open up to when I bow. What I describe in my book is how it works for me. If you wish to substitute my words of reflection and communion with your own, then of course that is fine.

Q83. *You speak about the Dharma Mind and pure awareness. Are they the same thing?*

A. No. Dharma Mind is the mind we nurture through practice. We are profoundly conditioned into always wanting and becoming something. 'I will do this because I want that' is the normal everyday mind that we are all familiar with. This is called the 'worldly mind'. The Dharma Mind is quite different. Through years of practice, we slowly, and with much patience, turn away from that wanting mind and learn to stop becoming (something), so beginning to awaken to the unconditioned Dharma Mind that neither wants or wants to become. Learning to let go of all those desires and aversions, you begin to be just as you are, in all situations. This letting go is called unbecoming. When the Dharma Mind is fully mature, you will be empty of self and attachment, and you will have returned to your childhood innocence. It's at this moment the Dharma Mind will collapse and vanish, and you will awaken to your true nature, which is your intrinsically pure awareness.

Q84. *You seem to speak in terms of there being something divine in all of us and life, and that opening up to this divine is an important part of practice. This seems to be a different orientation to just seeing into the emptiness of self, coming to see oneself as no more than an ever changing stream of conditions, etc. I wonder if as ex-Christians practising the Dharma we are in danger of dumping this openness to the divine along with our dumping of God, and how damaging this is to our understanding of practice and going for refuge.*

A. Seeing oneself as a stream of conditions is the smashing of the blinding barrier of self-view. With this done, the ultimate human birthright of returning to inconceivable

Buddha nature awaits. But for the return to our original nature to reach fulfilment, we need first to have nurtured a practice that goes beyond just discovering the illusion of self. Whilst practising over the years we need to nurture an opening up to our true nature by acknowledging that there is 'something' beyond the conscious sense of 'me'. Learning to open up and to hand that sense of self, with all its views and opinions and self-interest, into that mysterious unknown. Bowing, for example, is a wonderful and profound opportunity to practise going for refuge by coming together, familiarizing and communing with that warmth and mystery beyond 'me', and learning to trust and be carried by that 'which isn't me'. If you are not prepared to acknowledge 'that which you will never know', your understanding and release from suffering will not be complete. There can be just the understanding of emptiness of self, but realizing true emptiness goes way beyond that small 'victory'. True emptiness expresses itself through the warmth of the human heart, which when truly liberated is all that is. It is infinite compassion and love, it is wisdom, beyond birth and death, and eternal. If we do not learn to open up to this mystery and nurture this truth in our everyday commitment to practice, then we will surely miss out on the inconceivable liberation.

Q85. *I had an unusual experience recently that I wonder if you could comment on. I had been in a rather busy city for a number of days when suddenly I noticed a significant change in how I was feeling come over me. I suddenly became more present, with a feeling of spaciousness and ease. It was so tangible and not due to any* *conscious cultivation on my part that I stopped to look around and see what was going on. It was then that it dawned on me that for the previous few minutes I'd been standing next to a waterfall (albeit man made). I can't help but feel that I accidentally happened on something important, but don't quite know exactly what.*

A. Maybe your experience showed you how close you really are to that which is beyond our normal entrapment of self-perception. In those moments you lost your self and tasted the spaciousness and freedom that is so close to us, yet we rarely experience it. Usually we are looking somewhere else for release from this self-confinement, and never realize that we are actually living out of that freedom each and every moment. Maybe your experience of the waterfall brought upon you the quietness of mind that sometimes allows us to glimpse the tranquillity of our true nature.

The Teacher

Q86. *Do you think the inherited Buddhist teacher/pupil model needs rethinking as more western teachers emerge, or do you think we have misunderstood this relationship? Do we need to re-vision our ideas of teachers to prevent unhelpful expectations and projections occurring, or is this inevitable?*

A. I don't know exactly what you mean when you say we may have misunderstood the teacher/student relationship. I can only give my view of what must surely be the most important feature to anyone that aspires to a deep and meaningful practice of the path.

We are encouraged to reflect on the Arya Sangha. Those historical beings, from whom we draw inspiration and guidance, all had teachers. Even the Buddha himself had teachers. The many Buddhist traditions have their own interpretations of the Dharma, and schools within traditions still further interpretations. Yet there is at least one teaching they all agree upon, and that is a newly initiated Buddhist practitioner not only has a teacher, but they should be together for at least 5 years. How can serious modern devotees of the Way ever doubt this essential fact for correct practice? How can anyone seriously believe that it is possible to somehow grow into the depths of insight without a teacher? In my view only the conceit of the western mind could think there may be another way for deep meaningful practice, despite this overwhelming evidence of 2500 years of Buddhist practice.

In broad terms, it seems that the alternative model to the traditional one mentioned above, could be described as a 'horizontal' model. In this, you practise with others that are more or less on a par with your own understanding and also with those that may have some more experience but who would never be classified as being 'teachers' in the conventional sense. This creates an environment of equality where dangers such as abuse of power are negated. However, the whole structure of spiritual hierarchy that underpins the traditional 'vertical' approach is dispensed with.

There is a view held by many in the west that the relationship between student and teacher is as much to do with power as anything else. When you have trust and faith in a teacher firmly in place you have the basic requisite for what can be a very profound and far-reaching practice. During difficult times of practice, with trust and support you can begin to learn to let go of yourself and all your attachments. This can evoke fear and many other types of emotions, but now you can learn to stay with these experiences, something not possible before you had a teacher. Trust when the teacher says, 'Everything will be OK, open and let go'. You feel supported and may now be in a position to experience the letting go of your precious possessions. This is the aspiration of all Dharma practitioners. We are always going into the unknown in practice and that will always evoke fear in some form or another. By definition, we cannot know the unknown. Therefore, how can we know what is the best thing to do? We will inevitably wander off the path without a teacher's indispensable support. We will get it wrong.

Another feature of the student/teacher relationship is one of respect and deference. To be always giving yourself up to that person who you recognize as having more spiritual maturity is seen as the opportunity to develop humility and openness. In a traditional ordained sangha there is always a very clearly defined hierarchy in place to help nurture this habit still further beyond your teacher.

To the cynic, hierarchy will be seen as yet another opportunity for power games. However, very complicated forms of hierarchy have been put in place by the wise over the centuries, and these are there to undercut the will to power and encourage surrender and deference, not to mention mindfulness. Hierarchy in all situations throughout the day helps nurture the humility that is necessary for genuine spiritual change to take place, necessary for the breakthrough to our Buddha nature. Hierarchy is a very profound and indispensable feature of practice. It is the major component that helps create the 'vertical' framework, yet it is put to one side by the 'horizontal' system.

Hierarchical relationships are crafted so there is always a 'space' between you and your teacher, and you and others in your sangha. In that space sticky worldly attachments are avoided, as these can distract and impede the practice to a very serious degree. A 'horizontal' sangha runs the danger of becoming 'worldly'. These are like the relationships you had before you came to the practice, self-driven and filled with self-satisfying emotions. The space (or gap) that a 'vertical' form gives is exemplified by your relationship with your teacher, who you may attach to through ingrained habits, but they will never attach to you! It is a space that is clean, wholesome and non-threatening, and in which you practise the Dharma. You can learn to get familiar and play with the practice in this space without being overtaken by attachments to others. To dispense with the teacher and the qualities of hierarchical sangha is to 'throw the baby out with the bath water'. In my view it is as serious as that. In my view also, this will not produce deep spiritual insight, and those that practice in this alternative 'horizontal' environment could never go on to become spiritual teachers of any substance, fulfilling the need in our western Buddhist world for such precious beings.

Humility, surrender, deference, hierarchy. Wow, such words! We westerners don't need all that kind of stuff! I invite the reader to point to any historical saint, bodhisattva, or whatever you wish to call such beings in Buddhism, who has not learnt and cultivated these virtues, primarily through a teacher, before their breakthrough. I doubt that it has ever happened. Yet we are prepared to marginalize the student/teacher relationship and try something else.

We rationalize not having teachers because so many have abused their power and are corrupt. This is true. But the Dharma path is fraught with many dangers, not just corrupt teachers. That is the nature of what we do. If you are burning to see the Dharma, then you will need to take the risk.

We do have a very big dilemma in the west in that so many wish to practise seriously the whole of the path, but there simply are not the teachers to go around. But you the reader need not be put off by this. Go and find one in the tradition that attracts you, even if you have to travel far. It is true not everyone has the luxury, the opportunity to go searching, due to their circumstances in life. This is unfortunate. If this applies to you, then find the best situation for yourself and apply yourself wholeheartedly. Much change can still take place; much of the self can still fall away.

Q87. *I am interested on your views about needing 'support' on the path. You strongly emphasis the need for a teacher and sangha to really uncover reality. However, my experience of vipassana meditation is that it strengthens my self-confidence and self-reliance, and I feel both less trusting and less needing of the views of others. I find that I begin to instinctively know what to do, and actually communicating with others about deep meditation experience is rather counter-productive. I can understand the value of a very experienced teacher, but let's face it, most western sanghas are littered with wrong views and misinterpretations of what the Buddha was pointing to. Are these 'support' mechanisms really so important?*

A. Among the many virtues of a teacher and a sangha is they act as a counter-balance to check and reaffirm that you are practising correctly and are really on the path. There is, I can assure you, only one thing worse than being lost and confused in practice, and that is being convinced you are on the path when in fact you are well off it. The self and the accompanying delusions are so clever and so subtle that there isn't a person alive, short of being fully enlightened, that can truly know if the path is being correctly pursued. Even those who have returned to their original nature and clearly see reality can still unwittingly wander off, all this being due to the clever subtleties of the remnants of self. Always be on your guard when you say to yourself 'this is it!' The Buddha (teacher) and the sangha are two thirds of the triple gem and are not an option in practice if you wish to tread the Buddha's path wholly and correctly. They are there to see you walk this path, a journey that requires such subtle perception (the word 'subtle' actually doesn't really do justice to the refinement of practice that is necessary).

If you are convinced that you don't need the complete support of practice, you can join the large band of practitioners here in the west who are like-minded, and I look forward one day to listening to their stories of breaking of the root of becoming and going beyond rebirth. Self-reliance and confidence is very important, but be very careful with thinking that your convictions need no airing or challenge. The mind is very clever. Not for nothing have we all been wandering lost in samsara since time began.

Q88. *Is there a danger in reflecting on the tilakkhanas that one may not be emotionally positive enough to face what it is that these are telling us, and meet with negativity? Is there a danger that one may take on this practice too early on one's path, or is it never too soon? Should one be doing this practice without the support of a sangha or access to a teacher that themselves have made the journey?*

A. The great advantage of using the lakkhanas in practice is that they have infinite levels of contemplation. To take on the basic truths of existence – that everything is impermanent, unsatisfactory and not-self – can be seen as laying down an important part of the framework of practice anyway. So just to become familiar with them through reading and study, then superficially noticing the truth of these signs in our experience of life is a good and useful beginning.

The result of a deeper insight contemplation is that it breaks up the tightly held view of a permanent self, as it reveals that life as experienced is really no more than a collection of conditions that are in perpetual change. This undermines the firmly held belief of a permanent 'I', which most of us are convinced we are. If a deeper insight practice using the lakkhanas is used before we are ready for such revelations, it could quite easily have a disastrous effect on our mental well-being. In order to ensure we are ready for such profound insights we first need to put in place a proper framework of practice that is honed and fashioned over a good period of time. To make sure we do this properly, we should if at all possible take on a teacher who has made the journey themselves, who will instruct and guide whilst we build this framework. A sangha should also be in place, as this will act as a support and barometer as our developing understanding of the Dharma and practice deepens.

Q89. *Some spiritual paths emphasize practitioners receiving assistance (i.e., teachings, blessings, energy, etc.) from non-physical spiritual beings to help their meditation practice. For example, in the Taoist and Tibetan Buddhist paths, deities, bodhisattvas and* *yidams are utilized and are believed to exist (relatively speaking). What's your angle on this? As I understand the Dharma, one is generally encouraged to be independent and not rely on these external beings at all.*

A. The practice of the Dharma is full of skilful means on offer from the various traditions and schools that help us to engage in practice, when we are finding it very difficult to put into effect. Calling on the assistance of a deity is one example. Several traditions use them, with the Tibetan tradition the most prolific. We all need help and support, usually quite a lot of the time, in practice, and this highlights the importance of a teacher. The deities can be taken as teachers and have other functions as well when engaged with skilfully. They also have many of the qualities that we need to aspire to in order to break the delusion of self. All skilful means are a means to an end, not the end itself, and the use of deities can be a very potent one.

In the context of Buddhism, to me 'independence' means not to attach to the world and the unwise, but provisionally attach to the skilful means (wisdom) of Buddhism. It would be impossible to go beyond suffering without doing this to some degree.

Q90. *There are spiritual paths which believe it is important to receive 'transmission' from a guru or spiritual guide (i.e., blessings, energy, etc.) to help meditation practice. For example in some Hindu, Tibetan and Sufi paths, as I understand the situation, the student 'surrenders' and allows the teacher to 'open them up' spiritually using their psychic powers so they can have spiritual experiences. Again, what's your angle on this, and do you think it's a* *safe and effective method of practice? Is this part of the Theravada tradition?*

A. I can only talk from my own experience, and that was to have trust and faith in my teacher and, to the extent that I could, muster up courage to let go of my defences, opening myself to the Dharma that was offered. This I found had immense benefits. I would suggest that so called 'psychic power' is simply the clear vision of a teacher who, no longer blinded by ignorance, can see what is the right teaching for you at any given time. They cannot prise you open like a can opener. It's only when you surrender your entire being with trust that transmission can take place. If you can find someone who you can trust in this profound way, then you would surely discover this to be the best way to practise the Dharma. You empower your teacher by your surrender, but there is always the danger that the teacher will misuse this power. This is the risk you take. It is your decision.

This type of spiritual relationship is accepted in all traditions, but not, from my knowledge, particularly emphasized in Theravada.

Q91. *In order for authentic practice to occur, must one's teacher have attained to the first bhumi?*

A. Finding the right teacher can be a bit of a strange and mysterious experience, because I think it is more of an organic and subjective phenomenon than checking someone's 'credentials'. I believe that 'affinity links' can, and often do, play a major part as we reconnect with someone we once trained with before this life. To me it is much more a feeling that we have found the right person, and that we have the confidence to trust and surrender to their greater wisdom and teaching. A teacher is someone you are able to say yes to when they suggest you do something you are not sure of or are afraid of doing. How much you are able to trust the helping hand of your teacher in your opening to the unknown is the best touchstone by which to judge.

Q92. *Can spiritual practice (meditation, being in the now, etc.) in itself ever be enough to deliver insight? When I hear people speak so often about their spiritual practice, and even spiritual experiences, they sound very 'self-seeking' and seem to be caught up in the movement of time. Does true transformative practice need to be based in spiritual vision that has seen through the world to a certain extent, and a consequential letting go of it? If so, if one hasn't reached this point, can any amount of practice ever deliver anything substantial beyond giving the practitioner more 'stuff' with which to create an identity?*

A. If people are really 'self-seeking', then the whole process of practice becomes extremely questionable. If they really are in this state of mind, then all that is going to change is their ego as it becomes ever more deluded and entrenched. Actually, people in this state of 'practice' will never really enter the transforming process anyway. One of the greatest traps that we westerners fall into is that in our desire for change, we think it is the self itself that needs to do the changing. If we understand Dharma to be like this, then it is extremely doubtful that any sort of meaningful change could ever take place.

It is crucial to be able to tell the difference between doing something in order to gain, and doing something as 'skilful means'. Skilful means encourage and lead us to letting go, not only of the delusion of 'me and mine', but also of the 'skilful means' itself, which is helping us to let go. There is yet another form of practice that doesn't even encourage working with any of the Buddhist 'skilful means' at all, but rather points straight to letting go of our attachments.

I don't believe it is possible to engage correctly with any form of practice without a teacher, at least for a good few years. We will inevitably get it wrong, as we are so conditioned into doing something in order to get something in return. Spiritual practice is paradoxical, with spiritual understanding even more so. We need to see that although there is an apparent 'self-seeking', 'doing' motivation, we are in fact always nurturing the spirit of letting the practice go – we are not being deceived into attaching to the practice. This apparent contradiction can only be guarded against with the skilful engagement of a teacher who sees these dangers.

Q93. *How does a practitioner balance the need for a teacher and the need to be 'a light unto yourself'? Since Dharma practice leads one towards ever greater self-reliance, what role does a teacher have in one's insight and progress in Dharma?*

A. We are always going into the unknown when we embark upon the path. So by definition we cannot know how to walk this path with any sort of clarity, hence the need for a teacher. Like a teacher of any discipline, they teach us something we are unfamiliar with. Through familiarity and experience we begin to understand how we can continue to walk into this great unknown mystery we call the path.

Through faith and trust we tread the path supported by our teacher, but in time, and through experience, we gain the confidence to take the trip with less and less guidance. We discover through experience to identify the features of the path and how our relationship to them is cultivated. In the end we may well reach a point when we no longer need guidance at all. That will be a long way off, some say this point is only reached when the fetter of doubt is cut (stream entry) and the path becomes truly clear. But even then a wise being and someone who you trust may still be consulted, for the path still has dangers to be awakened to.

Q94. *Can we say, in a sense, that a traditional teacher will not get 'personal'? Rather, they will show you a possible way out or through your difficulty simply by talking Dharma. That way you do not feel judged or belittled (or indeed favoured), and the rest is up to you.*

A. Certainly not. Of course the teachings are very important, but if that is all that is needed, then why the need for a teacher? An authentic teacher, depending on circumstances, will use whatever skilful means needed to help guide and support you. To be able to show many 'faces' is the mark of an authentic teacher. He or she may display their wisdom in a straightforward way to help you let go of something that is blocking your own innate wisdom. They may equally challenge your position in a very personal way by exposing your views and actions that are responsible for your own blind spots and attachments.

I heard a story of one of the great forest masters of the Theravada tradition of Thailand, who ridiculed one of his disciples in a very personal way in front of the whole sangha in order to shake him out of a deep attachment, to which he was blind. If we read some of the many accounts of the Zen masters, we see they would often use physical teachings to challenge the fixed position of their disciples. To strike their students, even throw them into the river, displayed their limitless compassion and freedom in helping their students break through their impasses.

Q95. *I've read that the Buddha in discussion with Ananda cited spiritual friendship as being 'The whole of the spiritual life'. In certain quarters this seems to be taken to mean interpersonal relationships amongst spiritual practitioners and the dynamic of these relationships providing grist-to-mill of spiritual practice. Another interpretation of the statement that I've come across is that it is 'friendship with all that is beautiful in life' that the Buddha was speaking about, this being used to counter claims that Buddhism is a cold, distant and nihilistic 'religion'. I wonder if you care to share what you think the Buddha may have been getting at in regard to this. What would you say is meant by spiritual friendship?*
A. Let us first read the quote from the short *Upaddha Sutta* found in the *Samyutta Nikaya XLV.2*, which I think you are quoting.

> ...Ananda approached the Buddha, paid homage, sat down to one side, and said, 'Lord, this is half of the holy life, that is, good friendship, good companionship. Good comradeship.'

> 'Not so, Ananda! Not so, Ananda!' replied the Buddha, 'This is the entire holy life, Ananda, that is, good friendship, good companionship, good comradeship. When a bhikkhu has a

good friend, a good companion, a good comrade, it is to be expected that he will develop and cultivate the Noble Eightfold Path.'...

To my way of thinking there are two key words here, 'holy' and 'expected', which we need to explore so as to understand better the meaning of this sutta.

I was a Theravada novice monk for a few years and I often heard that being a monk was to lead the holy life. But how exactly was this defined? To many, simply to don the saffron robes was enough to fulfil that ideal, but to most monks it meant a whole lot more.

There are around 250 rules for monks to follow coupled with countless minor 'rules' that help them not only to stay within the main body of rules but refine still further the very basis of the monastic life, which is to nurture detachment from our tendency to grasp at life. These are the many little pointers that encourage the monk to build an optimum state of being, an optimum state of consciousness conducive to the unfolding of insight. This very refined way of living cannot successfully be put in place when pursued alone, if for no other reason than much of what they need to refine involves interaction and consideration for their fellow bhikkhus and community. Having a good friend, being given support, consideration and kindness, as well as being inspired by their company and exemplary conduct, becomes the bedrock of the holy life.

From this platform the monk is then expected to 'develop and cultivate the Noble Eightfold Path'. That is, practise the complete Dharma path. Apparently two separate pursuits?

Possibly so. They can be separated. A monk can just pursue the holy life and become a good respectful person with high ethical standards as well as being kind and helpful. But another whilst pursuing the holy life can move more deeply into the practice of the eightfold path.

I have met and have known fine monks that many would consider without hesitation to be leading the holy life, who have had no inclination to practise the whole of the eightfold path at all. Sila yes, but that is all. Fine, ethical, kind beings that may study and preach and do fine work in their community and temple, but have never pursued meditation and the cultivation of wisdom into the reality of their own being. So leading the holy life and being a good friend cannot be seen as the complete picture of the spiritual path.

Beyond these thoughts there is yet another consideration that can be brought to this sutta, and that is the hierarchical structure that permeates the sangha, which must provide the 'backdrop' to so many of the teachings of the Buddha. Try to imagine the make-up of the bhikkhu sangha at the time of the Buddha. From what we are told there were possibly hundreds if not thousands of sotapannas and attained bhikkhus up to the final attainment of arahatship. We read that many of these awakened monks had their own disciples (Shariputra is said to have had 500). Imagine (if you can!) this seemingly countless number of teacher/student relationships. So many spiritual hierarchical 'pyramids' that led from the student up to the teacher. These spiritual structures in turn formed the one main all-embracing pyramid that led to its peak, the Buddha himself. But there was yet another hierarchical structure.

There is the structure of the elders. A monk, once ordained, fits into this structure. This structure has nothing to do with spiritual authority gained from awakening. So, for example, an arahat would show deference to a monk ordained before him.

So we have two forms of hierarchy that ran through the entire structure of the sangha. One spiritual, and the other based on seniority. Hierarchy is integral to all religions and spiritual paths. Why the emphasis?

All spiritual paths focus on the self, and how it alienates us from the ultimate, whatever we may consider that to be. All spiritual paths aim to transform or pacify or eliminate this experience we call 'self'. The nature of self is conceit, and self-importance. Therefore hierarchy helps the monk to tackle this conceit and self-importance by training to surrender continually that conceit through various disciplines. To bow, to show deference to elders, for example, is a very skilful reminder to the monk that he is giving up this 'I'. Of course, there are other practices to cultivate on the spiritual path as well, but this form of practice is with the monk all the time throughout the day and in all activities. If this element of the spiritual path were not important, why have all religions throughout time and over the entire world used it?

Any interpretation of this section of this sutta that ignores the dual hierarchical structure that was obviously (so obvious that the Buddha didn't even bother to mention it) at the very heart of his definition of the holy life and spiritual friendship would show a lack of understanding of the whole picture. To ignore this guiding principle of spiritual friendship would create such an inaccurate and one-sided interpretation of the Buddha's teaching as to deprive it of any real significance.

Footnote: Most of what you read in the Pali Canon is for the ordained monk. The so-called holy life is letting you know that it is not possible for a layman to cultivate some of the more refined aspects of Buddhist practice. In my Theravada days I often heard this expression holy life used to let the congregation know, in a somewhat coded way, that there is a definite (superior) space between the ordained and the lay, so we should always remember that. Assertions like this convinced me of my love for Mahayana, where no such distinctions exist.

To answer your last question: You are suggesting this sutta could be a way of expounding spiritual friendship. I think you can do this to a degree as long as you realize that a friendship that is 'spiritual' is not the same as any other type of friendship. Other friendships, however sincere and skilful, nearly always carry attachments that by nature will have self-interest and are karma producing – even if we consider our actions towards such friends as being 'selfless'. Genuine spiritual friendship has non-attachment as its main characteristic – to help your friend without self-interest and attachments. A very difficult ideal to pursue and perfect, and quite impossible without a mature practice of the eightfold path in place. This then may imply more of a teacher/student relationship, but I don't think this is the teaching of this sutta. In fact, as I well remember from my days as a samanera in Sri Lanka, the general consensus in the sangha was that the authentic spiritual friend could only be either the Buddha or one of the arahats, as these are the only beings whose training has finished and are therefore qualified to teach. I always thought this was a bit of an extreme view, as that would only leave most of us without any 'genuine' guidance at all.

Personal Choices

Q96. *How important is chastity for practice and going for refuge in general?*

A. I don't understand how you can make a distinction between practice and going for refuge.

A major characteristic of the practice of the Buddha-Dharma is restraint, so that we may cultivate the ability to walk the middle way. When we truly alight and stay on the middle way – which is the perfection of the fourth noble truth – samsara will fall away to reveal our true nature. Restraint applies to all our attachments to views and opinions, desire and aversion, etc. Restraint means to keep in control, not deny or suppress. If we suppress, we may not only get ourselves into emotional trouble, but also deny ourselves the opportunity to get to know ourselves and work and make friends with what we are.

Of all our attachments it has to be said for most of us the desire for sexual fulfilment is the most powerful and difficult to control. For this reason it could be justified to break the rule of restraint, and contain to the extent of suppression, in the full knowledge that this act is only a temporary expedient. Yes, it can help, because of the massive emotional involvement that this aspect of our being seems to demand, and if you are successful in using this temporary expedient it probably is something useful to bring to the practice when you consider it necessary. But it is not necessary to go down this route in our pursuit of insight. To contain, and find the balance that is the middle way, applies to the sex drive in exactly the same way as to any other part of our make-up. Try celibacy if you so wish, but if you find it too difficult to maintain, better to give it up than maybe do yourself some psychological damage, consider yourself a failure, and even give up the practice as well. To practise the middle way is the way to nirvana, and if your sexual drive is a part of your mandala of practice, then so be it.

Q97. *In putting my 'nose to the grindstone and working with what's in front of me', one of the largest areas of practice for me has been working with sexual desire. I've come to realize that if I could put even a little of the time and effort I invest in sexual fantasy and desire (every few minutes) into Dharma practice, I'd have a very consistent practice indeed. Once I get caught up in these lustful states I find it very difficult to maintain any kind of awareness and sometimes don't even want to. These are strong habitual tendencies that cause me a lot of confusion and distress. Any advice? Thanks.*

A. Your experiences are very common to practitioners, especially men, I would suggest. I myself had similar experiences to work with for many, many years. First thing you need to do is try and accept that this is the way you are, and don't make a problem out of it by engaging in dialogue and beating yourself up with mental conflict. For whatever reason, you are like this, so try and accept and make friends with it. Not easy I know, but I know no other way forward.

Speaking from my own experiences, I always tried to incorporate my sexual drive, when it appeared during sitting, into my daily practice of containment, understanding and insightful meditation; and I would maintain awareness, investigate this almost uncontrollable drive, even during the physical act of fulfilling my sexual desires.

This drive seems to be the most basic and unfathomable aspect of the human make-up. Most things that go to make us up we can usually get to the bottom of, or at least make good inroads into, but the urge for sex, from my experience, is a chasm that has no parameters. After years of trying to work out why I was like this, I finally learned to accept that maybe I was never going to truly understand, and so I let go of trying. When I finally gave up trying, maybe it was then that I found the best clue to the answer. There was the discovery that my sexual desire/drive was always at its strongest when I felt lonely and insecure, and much more in the grip of fear.

We can work on fear, which manifests in countless mental and emotional forms, through the correct practice of the path. I discovered that in time and through the transforming process of practice, fear generally began to subside and die, and I noticed that my attachment to sexual desires also began slowly but surely to diminish.

Q98. *Do you believe that living in a single-sex environment is conducive to Dharma practice? Some Buddhists feel that the presence of the opposite sex causes a kind of 'projection' which prevents*

*one from integrating all their psychological forces. Do you feel this
sort of thing has anything to do with the Dharma at all?*
A. Segregation of the sexes has been at the centre of most, if
not all, religions throughout time, so we have to accept that
there is maybe something conducive to the spiritual path in
participating in this way of living. In Buddhism celibacy has
always been central to all traditions, so therefore keeping
the sexes apart has been necessary. For most of us the sex
drive is the major distraction on the path. It can so easily
consume our thoughts, promoting a powerful emotional
drive that is extremely difficult to contain. In this context to
be carried away by this power is not skilful; it can so easily
lead us from the path and cement us even more in the world
of all-consuming attachment.

The power of the sex drive to divert us from our aspirations may have been the main reason for the segregation of
the sexes over the centuries. Or maybe it's because maintaining a social discipline of order would have not been possible in anything other than a single-sex situation. Maybe
it's a combination of the two.

These are skilful tools used on the spiritual path. But that
is what they are, tools. It is not necessary to be celibate to
practise the path. Living a life that includes the opposite sex,
or even your own sex, and may include engaging in intimate relations doesn't by definition diminish the insightful
path to liberation. It may well make the path more difficult
to follow. But if our desires and attachments around something that involves the natural urge to procreate can be in-
corporated in a skilful way, it can become a powerful vehicle

to insight. Fraught with many dangers, maybe, but definitely possible.

Q99. *I have some major issues with intimacy in my life (and fear of intimacy). It seems that intimacy with myself is as much a part of this as intimacy with other people. Could you say something about this, please?*

A. Here we have the very basis of our human predicament, the relationship that we have with ourselves. It is precisely this predicament that Dharma addresses and cures. We create duality soon after birth and from there we create a relationship with ourselves, the quality of which depends on many and varied conditions. As individuals we learn to live with that relationship, but those of us that are not satisfied with it look for remedies to make it better. Dharma practice can be defined in many ways, but for me the most human and accessible definition is to consider it to be a practice of making friends with ourselves. In fact it goes further and says rather than making friends with ourselves we learn to love ourselves. It is a practice that brings together the many conflicting dualities that we are. While we engage in the practice of Dharma we slowly awaken to the truth that the relationship we have with ourselves and our relationships with others actually mirror one another, and we begin to see self and other as not being two, but actually one. We then come to the obvious conclusion that if we like ourselves, we cannot help but like others. In fact, it will be impossible for that not to be. The late well-known and respected Sri Lankan monk Anandamitreya once said, 'You cannot love someone until you love yourself – it's impossible'. Your predicament with intimacy with others is a mirror of your relationship with yourself. Practise the Dharma and learn to go beyond duality, and you will not only be intimate with yourself and others, but the whole of life.

Q100. *What do you do when feeling all needy and wanting some-one to hug and hold you? Sometimes it seems that we Dharma-farers must be stoic and mindful, staying with whatever is going on, not running from it into the arms of a comforting friend. Where on this noble path, the place for hugs and holding, the loving and accepting of sorrow, sadness, loneliness? Isn't the self and self-pity at the root of all sorrow and not to be encouraged? Should the strong emotions from which the self arises be not indulged in at any cost? What do you do when blue?*

A. Sangha and a teacher will help you bear with your emo-tions to a large extent, but when they are too powerful in the way you describe them, for example, find a friend and a shoulder to cry on. Let go, but try to observe the precepts as best you can. We can only do our best; no-one can contain all the time in all situations. What is important here is to make friends with what you perceive to be your limitations and not get into negative thoughts about not being capable of doing the practice. Don't beat yourself up; be kind and considerate to yourself and your present condition. Re-member, we are all trapped by karma so entrenched that no one can let go by an act of will, and the process of change can be very emotional and fearful. Be gentle, but be firm and committed, so when the situation arises again you do your best to bear with just that little bit more than the last time. And no, self-indulgence is never a good thing.

Q101. *I wonder if you could say some more on attachment and how it holds us back from progress along the path. In particular, can you say something about it in relation to desire, or thirsting after things? I've understood that it is desire for things which is an obstacle, and that one's Dharma practice ideally leads to greater contentment and doing without. However, if I understand recent postings by you, it is more the emotional attachment that we place on objects that hinders, and that desire itself may or may not be something that we can't do a lot about (you don't say this, I'm speculating). I can see how overcoming desire and overcoming attachment can both lead to contentment, stillness, doing without, etc. However, it seems to me that perhaps the nature or focus of practice is different in each case. For example, if I'm attempting to overcome my tendency to desire things, I may well decide to remain out of a relationship and be stoic about this. However, if it's attachment that is the 'devil', it's the attachment to my partner and wanting the relationship to be a certain way that now becomes the practice ground; being in a relationship is of itself perfectly natural and Dharmically acceptable.*

A. Becoming unattached IS the path. Outside of attachment there is no world and therefore no suffering. In a metaphysical sense we are attached moment by moment, even when we are at our most peaceful. But we can hardly do anything about that. What we can address are our obvious attachments that manifest through the emotions. We focus on containing and working with them. This then becomes the transforming process that characterizes the Mahayana.

You could say there are two perspectives on containment practice: Restraint before the event takes place, and restraint when the event is in play. The first is to restrain or even deny something we are strongly attached to (or maybe see it as something that may hinder the practice). The second is to live life and, if you so wish, knowingly (if not willingly) take on something that you are attached to, then see it as your training ground. To use your example, if you feel you can live without a relationship, because you know it will certainly bring dukkha in one form or another and make your practice much more difficult to do, then restrain yourself from entering into it. If you feel you don't want to/can't live without a relationship, then that is OK as well. You are taking on a form of practice that for you will be difficult to fulfil, but do it anyway. It could be your vehicle to awakening. Or maybe it will be your vehicle to even greater dukkha. Either way, emotional restraint IS the practice.

Q102. *I wonder whether you have any thoughts on the need for solitude for those going for refuge. How important is it for the spiritual seeker to experience aloneness, or for that matter, even loneliness? Is aloneness necessary for spiritual progress, and therefore should intimate, companion-type relationships be renounced?*

A. The aloneness of a retreat from time to time is essential for those going for refuge, for it is at times like these that we have the opportunity to get to know and understand ourselves to a degree not possible in our ordinary everyday lives. All Dharma practice is focused directly or indirectly on the human existential truth of loneliness, caused by the sense of separateness from what is.

When we are alone we can open up to that greatest of our fears whilst in its grip, and see directly into it. Here we may discover that if we learn to open and stay with loneliness, we will see it for what it is and learn to accept and make friends with it. Whilst on this journey of transformation we may come to see that everything that we have ever done in our lives is just a deep subconscious search by our own heart, bound by delusion, to be reunited with the totality of what is. Our onward journey into understanding loneliness need not exclude companion-type relationships, for this sort of experience may well show us just how lonely we basically are, and how difficult it is to live with and accept that truth.

Q103. *Because of my work, and having a baby daughter, at the moment I have practically no time to sit. But my train journey to work takes an hour each way, so I have started to use this time for meditation. I wonder though if the 'quality' (for want of a better word) is going to be a poor second to actually sitting in a quiet room? At present, this, and trying to spend the day mindfully, feels very useful, but I wonder if I am missing out on the 'furnace of attention' of formal zazen?*

A. To make use of your circumstances in the way that you are doing is a very skilful thing to do. Of course, to be able to sit regularly in a quiet room would be a better situation to be in, but that is not possible for you just now. In your case, having dependants gives you the golden opportunity to nurture the fundamental reality of Dharma practice, which is one of selfless action. To live your life for others who depend on you can open you up to yourself in a very direct way that is often denied to those of us who are single and don't have to live our lives for others. We single folk can easily become blinkered and fall into the trap of self-indulgence.

Q104. *Can the forum suggest a Dharma way to deal with being the object of another person's obsession? How does one deal with abusive mental attacks and the fear of such attacks, while at the same time remaining aware of all the many blessings one has in life? How does one warm up the heart, and keep it warm, so that it can withstand relentless abuse? I'm afraid of this person, and he will never let go. But I'm gonna live my life. What would the Buddha do? He always knew what to do. The Dharma will have a way. Can the forum see a way, please?*

A. I'm very sorry to read of your predicament but I don't think this is strictly a situation for Buddhism, at least in the short term. Buddhism is about learning about yourself and the change that takes place on that journey. That change should cultivate inner strength, so that we become the master of our situation rather than its victim. In a situation like yours, you become master in the sense that you don't allow yourself to be the abused, but rather have the courage and inner ability to become emotionally detached from the abuser and take charge of your own emotional experience. Inner strength gives us the ability even to walk away from the abuse and maybe start completely anew. This usually takes years of practice. I'm afraid there's no quick fix in Buddhism.

During the time of developing this inner strength through practice, one of the skills (upaya) we learn in order to help us through life is to employ other (external) measures, as and when needed. In this case I would employ someone outside of the situation to help, like a counsellor, or someone skilled in emotional abuse situations. Sometimes our experiences are just too powerful for us to deal with, and a part of Dharma practice is to admit that things sometimes are just too big for us right now. To acknowledge this truth can be a big step forward.

Q105. *Should the meditator be a teetotaller?*
A. I would suggest the following answer: If you happen to like alcohol, then, as always, walk the middle way. Alcohol dulls the senses and confuses our reality, so this is hardly conducive to meditation and an ethical practice. But then again, if we enjoy a bit of relaxation with a drink, best not to take ourselves too seriously and deny ourselves this small pleasure.

Q106. *I have some questions regarding practice. Perhaps I could ask through your website, so hope that is OK – one is about vegetarianism, which is an issue close to my heart!*
A. One of the great contentious issues in modern-day western Buddhism! Before I give you my personal thoughts, let me first give you a couple of examples from what I would consider as scriptural authority.

Devadatta (the cousin of the Buddha) told the Buddha there should be five more rules added to the fledgling code of conduct for bhikkhus. One of these five was that monks should no longer be permitted to eat meat or fish. The Buddha turned down this demand, stating monks should eat whatever is offered by the lay community. He said the only time they should refuse meat or fish from the laity was when it was killed for them; neither should they desire to kill for food themselves. The refusal of the Buddha to concede these demands led not only to the first schism in the sangha, but also led Devadatta, in his frustration at not being successful in starting his own sangha, to try to take the life of the Buddha.

In the time since the Buddha, vegetarianism has never been a practice in the Buddhist east except in the odd situation, usually inspired by an abbot or monastic teacher who wanted his place meat free. Even today, if you choose to go to any Buddhist country you will find meat and fish eating is a part of the daily diet of even the most ethical, devout and sincere Buddhists.

It is important to understand that the Buddha stated quite clearly that there are only two instances (cited above) when you would be karmically involved with killing. In avoiding those two instances you are not violating the natural law of things, thereby confirming that the path of practice is not blocked. This dispels the myth held to by many (western) Buddhists that you have to be vegetarian in order to practise the Dharma.

This leads to another very important consideration – but one for another time – that the very basis of Dharma practice is about accepting things the way they are, rather than trying to shape the world to how you think it should be. This is one of the subtlest insights of the Buddha and his teachings, and sets Dharma practice apart from most other spiritual traditions.

Having dealt with what would be considered factual points, this does leave much more to say. Personally, I have great respect for those who decide to be vegetarian and pursue what is seen by many as a deep ethical choice. This is such a strong issue for many that they would consider it inconceivable to try to practise and not be vegetarian. If there is such a strong feeling, then vegetarianism should be pursued, but remember to be careful to avoid the common trap of feeling spiritually superior to meat-eaters and parade yourself with your bright shiny moral badge. When this becomes the case, it can be just another possession reaffirming and reinforcing the sense of self.

These days, with the tendency in the west to vegetarianism, you may well find teachers that expect their students not to eat meat. If it is one of the conditions for joining a sangha, then you have to accept this and do your best to respect that expectation (maybe along with others that you disagree with), considering it as part of your practice. But on the other hand, if you find a teacher that refuses to teach you the Dharma and help you with your struggle in samsara because you are partial to sausage rolls, then you may want to ponder the depth of his compassion.

Q107. *Would you agree with the view that buying meat and fish are the same as eating something that has been killed for you – meat and fish are made available for consumers. If you buy it and eat it then all that you have done is avoided the messy business of*

killing by paying an anonymous person to do the work for you. So, doesn't buying meat and fish amount in practice to the killing?
A. No I wouldn't, and this view isn't held in Buddhism. We need to have some understanding of the important concept of the Pali/Sanskrit word cetana. Cetana is a very important concept in Dharma practice. Cetana means intention (will, action, volition) and it's our intention that creates karma and the world that we help to create and experience as being full of suffering. We as practising Buddhists focus on the part we play in that suffering and give unwavering attention to transforming our own cetana both for our own sake and for the sake of others. Observing the precepts helps to guide and support us whilst we work with our outflows (cetana) so we do our best to observe those precepts. In this case, as there hasn't been any direct involvement (cetana) with the death of an animal, cetana simply doesn't apply; we are not therefore violating the first precept. This is Buddhist wisdom.

The Buddha wasn't a vegetarian, nor his vast sangha, including countless arahats who, like the Buddha, had finished their training and gone beyond the creation of karma, reaching the pureness of thought, word and action. The numerous traditions that have sprung up in the east over the more than two thousand years since the Buddha have never been vegetarian, and I don't recall any of the prominent saints and sages of Buddhism saying that to follow the Dharma you must be vegetarian. To suggest, as many do in the west that the first precept is violated by eating meat is to suggest that all those who have practised traditional Buddhism, including the Buddha and the arhants, have been in violation of the first precept. I can best suggest you read the recent post concerning vegetarianism for my general view on the subject.

If you wish to create a 'moral' view for vegetarianism (or anything else), then it should be based first on the cultural background, and always be a personal view for you alone. Do remember, there will be many sincere spiritual people, and many fine human beings that don't have a spiritual path, who will disagree with whatever new ideas you come up with. That's why if you really seek guidance as to what is right and wrong it is best to stay with 'rules' that are part of the natural laws that govern nature, which are always conditioned by the laws of karma.

If we decide to set up new ideas and propagate them in the name of Buddhist morality, we will be setting up a duality, which will always create problems. This will inevitably bring conflict with those who disagree, thus violating the basic spirit of Buddhism, which is to accept things the way they are. Remember, never has there been a conflict in the name of Buddhism in 2500 years; do you think that fine record is in place through mere luck?

Q108. *How important is it to avoid killing insects? I'm usually happy 'rescuing' flies, wasps, bees, etc. when they come through my window, but I have problems with mosquitoes. They want my blood, and their bites are unhealthy. I find that if I don't squash them immediately they hide somewhere in my room and get me when I'm sleeping.*
A. As with all actions, it is your volition that is the important factor. To kill because one enjoys killing cannot be whole-

some, and will have its consequences. If it is your health that concerns you, then take one of the numerous precautions that are available, that way you won't have to kill them. Or you could reflect on metta and take the attitude that the mosquito has as much right to be here as you and let them have a spot or two of blood. It's very unlikely that you will come to any harm and it will surely give them a few moments of pleasure and fulfilment in a precarious life that is short and full of anxiety.

Glossary

Anattā: no-self or not-self

Aniccā: impermanence

Arhat: (Pali: *Arahat*) saint who has attained freedom from rebirth

Bhikkhu: ordained Theravada monk

Bodhisattva: enlightening being aspiring to full enlightenment by liberating all sentient beings

Bhūmi: stage of the bodhisattva path

Brahma Vihāras: the 'four sublime states of mind' meditation techniques

Dharma: (Pali: *Dhamma*) the teachings of the Buddha or the truth or reality

Dhyāna: (Pali: *Jhāna*) meditative stability or absorption

Dukkha: suffering or unsatisfactoriness

Hara: seat of the emotions and spiritual centre in the lower body

Hīnayāna: southern Buddhist schools or the so called 'lesser vehicle' schools

Mahāyāna: northern Buddhist schools or the so called 'great vehicle' schools

Māla: rosary

Maṇḍala: one's field of practice

Māra: 'the evil one', negative thoughts or emotions

Mettā Bhāvanā: loving kindness meditation – one of the Brahma Viharas

Mudrā: hand position

Nirvāṇa: (Pali: *Nibbāna*) the 'deathless', or unconditionality

Prajñā: (Pali: *Paññā*) wisdom

Pūjā: devotional ceremony

Samādhi: non-dualistic state of meditative experience

Sāmanera: novice monk of the Theravada tradition

Śamathā: (Pali: *Samatha*) meditation technique

Saṁsāra: the dualistic mind-made world of eternal becoming

Sangha: community of Dharma practitioners

Shikantaza: (Japanese) just sitting. The meditation practice of Soto Zen

Śunyatā: (Pali: *Suññatā*) the emptiness of self-nature in all things

Śīla: (Pali: *Sīla*) conduct or ethics

Sotapanna: stream-entry. The first stage of enlightenment

Śraddhā: faith

Sūtra: (Pali: *Sutta*) discourse of the Buddha

Tilakkhaṇa: the three signs of conditioned phenomena

Upāya: skilful means

Vipaśyanā: (Pali: *Vipassanā*) insight meditation practice

BY THE SAME AUTHOR

A RECORD OF AWAKENING

'The rare and inspiring example of a life consistently and uncompromisingly dedicated to the practice of the Dharma.'

Urgyen Sangharakshita

The remarkable fruit of more than twenty years' immersion in Buddhist practice: a practice that has been both deep and far-reaching.

In this book David Smith, 'an ordinary working-class chap' who came across Buddhism, shares his extraordinary inner experience. Taking us through his journey – from initial practice in the Zen tradition and three years as a Theravadin monk to his recent years as a lay practitioner in East London – he describes the basic principles of his practice and the process whereby the 'tap root of ignorance' is cut and the Awakened Mind is born.

His account reminds us that the Awakened Mind is within the reach of every one of us prepared to make the effort.

152 pages
ISBN 0-9542475-1-5
£7.99

AVAILABLE FROM ALOKA PUBLICATIONS

www.dharmamind.net

information@dharmamind.net

BY THE SAME AUTHOR

DHARMA MIND WORLDLY MIND

This is not a book of lists and formulas like so many books on Buddhist practice. Instead, it begins by creating a practical framework for understanding the principles of the Buddha's teaching, and then goes much further, offering valuable advice on how to put those principles into practice. It focuses not just on sitting meditation but more crucially on our daily lives. If we do not carry our Buddhist practice into daily life, the deep and permanent change that we all want will not be possible. David Smith offers his own personal insight, based on nearly 30 years of committed Dharma practice, on how to cultivate this most subtle and deeply profound path of transformation.

116 pages
ISBN 0-9542475-0-7
£7.99

AVAILABLE FROM ALOKA PUBLICATIONS

www.dharmamind.net

information@dharmamind.net